All N *Sings*

A Devotional Guide to Animals of the Bible

Ben Cooper

Ben Cooper

Psalm 105:2

ISBN 978-1-64416-994-0 (paperback)
ISBN 978-1-64416-995-7 (digital)

Christian Faith Publishing, Inc.
832 Park Avenue
Meadville, PA 16335
www.christianfaithpublishing.com

Printed in the United States of America

Endorsements

Dr. Woodrow Kroll of wkministries.com, *former President and Senior Bible Teacher for* **Back to the Bible** and creator of the **HELIOS Projects** *writes:*

All Nature Sings is unlike any book I have ever read. It has it all. If you want to learn something about the birds or animals mentioned in the Bible, you will. You'll also discover how many times and where that bird or animal is talked about in the Bible. And best of all, Ben Cooper has included spiritual insights gleaned from each of God's creatures that will encourage you in your daily walk with Jesus Christ. *All Nature Sings* is fun, factual, and for the whole family. Get a copy. You'll be glad you did.

Pastor Daren Ritchey of **Grace Bible Church**, Holidaysburg, PA writes:

Ben Cooper has combined his love for scripture and his love for God's creatures. The material in these pages is both informational and devotional. Children and adults will gain a greater appreciation for God's amazing creation after reading this book.

Contents

Acknowledgments

Many unending thanks to my great God and Savior, Jesus Christ, because without Him, none of this would be possible.

My wife, Sonia, and children for standing by me during my writing journey.

Thanks also go out to all the teachers, preachers, and speakers that have inspired me along my Christian life and study of the Bible.

Brenda Moore for her willingness to proofread and provide first draft edits.

Pastor Don Harrelson for doctrinal review.

Sandy Arnold, Wesley Cooper, and Suzanna Cooper for their animal artwork.

My church family and Christian friends for their prayers, encouragement, and patience.

Dr. Woodrow Kroll, Phil Robertson, and Pastor Daren Ritchey for their endorsements.

Preface

The Bible does not begin with a defense for proof of the existence of God. The Holy Spirit, working through men by the approval of God the Father, testifies to us the existence of God. Since God is, we need not question that He created the universe. In *Romans 1:19–20* we read,

> *Because that which is known about God is evident within them: For God made it evident to them. For since the creation of the world, His invisible attributes, His eternal power and Divine nature, having been clearly seen, being understood through what has been made, so that they are without excuse.*

This scripture is referred to as the "witness of creation." God is clearly seen in the things He has made. This is one of the essential thoughts behind the writings found within the pages of the Bible. Since God's word says His attributes, His eternal power, and His divine nature are all evident in the things He has made, we can examine those created things to get a glimpse of God and the truths pertaining to animals and the Bible. These are not opposite viewpoints left for man to line up on one side versus the other to spark heated debates. They both are truths that have been interwoven together as a tapestry to show the beauty and awesomeness of God and His majesty.

The Bible was not written to be a scientific textbook. However, all the scientific statements found within are true. Some skeptics would suggest that the Bible is not scientifically accurate. Yet slowly over the years, science is coming alongside of God's word. His word hasn't changed. More and more, science is supporting biblical statements. There are no conflicts. In fact, it would be a far better practice to blame any conceived error on man's inability to understand God's ways rather than fault God as being in error.

Many examples exist in history where man's failure to know the truth has been corrected by later discoveries that line up with God's word.

1. The earth is a sphere. *"It is He who sits above the circle of the earth"* (*Isaiah 40:22*). It wasn't all that long ago that man thought the world was flat and that if he traveled too far, he would fall off the edge of the world.

2. The earth is suspended in space. *"He stretches out the north over empty space, and hangs the earth on nothing"* (*Job 26:7*). The university that I attended still has a sculpture of the earth riding on the back of a very large tortoise depicting its means of travel through space. Other cultures suggest that a man upholds the world by his shear strength.

3. The sea has mountains and canyons. *"Then the channels of the sea appeared"* (*2 Samuel 22:16*). In the mid-1800s, it was common belief that the sea was bowl shaped. We have since learned by underwater exploration that channels and mountains exist in the oceans.

4. There are currents in the sea. *"Birds of the heavens and fish of the sea, whatever passes through the paths of the sea"* (*Psalm 8:8*). During a period of poor health, Matthew Maury had his son read scripture to him. One such day as he listened, his son read about paths in the sea. Maury was said to say that if God's word tells us there are pathways in the sea, he was going to find them. He is considered the father of oceanography for discovering and mapping the sea currents. A statue of Matthew Maury can be found in Richmond, Virginia, where he has maps in one hand and the Bible in the other.

5. All things reproduce after their kind (*Genesis 1:21*). Since He created every living thing after its kind, this would give credence that all things created will generally look like their parents and not by the process of evolution.

Why did God inspire men to include animals in the pages of scripture? Is not all scripture inspired by God as stated in *2 Timothy 3:16*? If the Creator of all things deemed it important enough to include animals in scripture, then this book is an attempt to consider His word and His created world to gain a deeper respect for the Author of life itself.

This book contains a selection of the animals found in the Bible and their references. It also contains unique background information on the species, including scientific and common names of animals that fit into those groupings. Most of the animal profiles in this book are species from North America. Each animal included has a "spiritual application" portion from my personal experiences and offers potential insight as to what God intended for us to learn from their inclusion in the Bible.

All Nature Sings was written to be used as background scientific information, sermon illustrations, personal devotions, and a reference for animals listed in the Bible. It is my sincere desire that reading this book will deepen your faith in the God who created you and everything around you.

> *All things were made through Him, and without Him*
> *was not anything made that was made. (John 1:3)*

The God of the universe desires to have a relationship with you, His creation. His word, the Bible, has been given to you so that you may know Him and His son, Jesus Christ, who came, lived among man, and was unjustly accused a sinner. He was unfairly judged and sentenced to die a death He did not deserve. But He did it willingly because God demanded a pure, sinless sacrifice for you to have a relationship with Him. He paid the price of your sin with His own life for you. And not just you only, but for the sins of the entire world— past, present, and future. Jesus died and was buried. If He were just an ordinary man, His story would end there. But Jesus wasn't an ordinary man. He was God in the flesh. Death could not keep Him. He died to defeat death. He rose from the dead, appeared to men, and left them to return to His rightful place with God in heaven. But before He left, He promised to come back for His church and will take those that believe back with Him forever. If you are not confident of your own personal salvation, today is a great day for you to surrender your life to Him.

And in the meantime, we wait. Not as ones sitting on a couch biding their time. By no means! We wait as those that have called upon the name of Jesus for salvation because we have work to do. Waiting, in this case, isn't passive. It's active! We are to be about our Father's business. Sharing the gospel with others! Helping those in need! Giving others the same eternal hope that abides in us!

Note: The title of this book comes from the first verse of an old hymn written by Maltbie Davenport Babcock that used to be sung in our churches. I wished it was still sung today. The evidence of our Creator is there if we take the time to look and listen for it.

This Is My Father's World

This is my father's world, and to my listening ears,
All nature sings and round me rings,
The music of the spheres.
This is my father's world, I rest me in the thought
Of rocks and trees and skies and seas, His hand the wonders wrought.

By the grace of God,
Ben H. Cooper

Ass (Equus asinus)

Common Name: Donkey

Background

The donkey is one of those animals you look at, take a step back, and scratch your head. It looks somewhat like a horse, but oddly different. It must be those long ears. One dictionary defines *donkey* in these ways:

1. A horse-like animal with large ears.
2. A stupid or obstinate person.

Donkeys can be used to ride on or to carry heavy loads. In either case, it won't take very long to figure out that they have a mind of their own. Like their cousin the mule, the donkey displays both a strong back and headstrong characteristics.

Growing up on the family farm, we usually had a donkey among the assortment of animals. They made good watchdogs and alarms. Often when a car drove in the driveway, the donkey would announce the arrival of a visitor with their traditionally loud trademark bray.

It was during my four-month college internship at the Heifer International Ranch, just north of Little Rock, Arkansas, where I got to see the stubborn side of the donkey used. They had one thousand heads of Brangus cattle, and one of my jobs was to halter-break the show cattle. Some of these animals were yearling heifer and bull calves weighing up to nine hundred pounds. Not all of them were eager to have a rope wrapped around their face and be forced to walk around in circles without giving resistance. That's when the donkey earned his keep.

The procedure was quite simple, but very effective. The unruly calf was tethered to the donkey with a line that fastened to the donkey's halter. Usually, the calf would jump, kick up its heels, and try to pull away from the donkey. The donkey did what came naturally to him—he remained stubborn. He would pull the slack out of the line by shifting his weight backward, keeping constant tension on the rope. Eventually, the calf would wear itself out and submit to the donkey's persistent pull. It always seemed to work because the donkey simply did what a donkey does.

The average life span of a donkey is twenty-five to thirty years. They are capable of producing offspring. However, a cross between a donkey and a horse, referred to as a mule, is sterile.

Scriptural Reference

The term "donkey" is never used in the King James Version of the Bible. Instead, all 153 references to this animal is an "ass." See appendix 3 for a list of the specific references.

Spiritual Application

Jesus chose to use a donkey's colt as the means to make His triumphal entry in the city of Jerusalem. And then tucked away in the Old Testament book of Numbers, this stubborn animal was used by God to speak to her human rider, a prophet for hire, because he was so obstinate that he couldn't even see the Angel of the Lord standing right in front of him. Let's zoom closer into this account found in the book of Numbers chapters 22 to 25.

Balak sent messengers three times to hire Balaam to pronounce a curse against the nation of Israel, who were infiltrating his territory. Balak and other leaders feared the Israelite God and were now seeing His chosen people coming through their land in multitudes. God spoke to Balaam and told him not to go. God finally told him if he was going to go, speak only what He would give him to say.

As Balaam traveled, there were three different occasions the way was blocked by the Angel of the Lord. Each time, the donkey saw the pre-incarnate image of Christ, but Balaam did not see anything. The pathway got rougher and narrower until the donkey could not move in any direction. She just sat down on the ground. Balaam took out a switch and beat the donkey to get her to move. Instead of moving, she reacted by speaking to Balaam. She told him she had carried him everywhere he needed to go for most of his life and had always obeyed him. All those trips she took him where he needed to go. It was only on this journey she refused because the Angel of the Lord was blocking the way. She implied that Balaam was so distracted by Balak's request that he could not see the presence of God at all. Balaam beat his donkey for not obeying him. Ironically, it was Balaam being stubborn and obstinate, not his donkey.

What can we learn from this supernatural account of a talking donkey? God's plans will not be altered. All His created things are at His disposal to accomplish His will. That even includes allowing the poster child of all stubbornness in the animal kingdom to be used to teach disobedient mankind that His divine plans will come to pass.

Numbers chapters 23 and 24 show us God's judgment on those that disobey Him. Balak wanted Israel to be cursed. But each time he moved Balaam to a different observation point, God instructed Balaam to bless Israel. Eventually, Balak was the one who was cursed. Often, God uses role reversal in His dealings with disobedient man. The disobedient desires within God's people cause unpleasant trials to be heaped upon themselves.

We think we know what is best. We climb up on our high horses and charge full steam ahead without ever seeking God's direction. We are foolish, stubborn, and cannot even see God right in front of us. He is right there trying to direct us on the way we should go. He loves us so much that He goes to great lengths to get our attention and set us back on course, even to the point of using a talking donkey to reveal our own stubbornness.

> *for they did not meet the people of Israel with bread and water, but hired Balaam against them to curse them—yet our God turned the curse into a blessing. (Nehemiah 13:2)*

Bear (Ursus americanus)

Common Name: Black Bear

Background

The North American black bear is a fascinating creature. As an avid beekeeper, one would think I would harbor ill feelings for bear. Even though I have had my share of run-ins with a couple, they are simply doing what they were created to do, eat! They have a driven propensity to eat as much as they can before the end of fall.

The black bear has some very unique character traits. Their mating season takes place in June. The fetus has a delayed implantation into the uterus until late fall when the female bear needs to be fattened up for her winter sleep. Black bears do not actually hibernate. They do slow their metabolism down and go into what is called a "deep sleep." If the mated female has not stored enough fat to meet her winter needs and that of the potential cubs she is carrying, her body will abort the fetuses for her own survival. Therefore, sows may only give birth eight times in the wild. They have this natural population control and self-preservation system within themselves.

The female bear wakes up to deliver her cubs and then slinks back off into her deep sleep. She responds to their cries and moves for her cubs to nurse. They will nurse for nearly a year. Once they become old enough to venture out of the den, they will begin to sample the same foods that the sow eats. This begins their training. Female cubs will stay with their mom for about eighteen months. While living in their family unit, she teaches her cubs where to find food, how to hunt and fish, and how to prepare for the winter.

The black bear has one of the longest nurturing periods of all the animals. Sows show care and affection to their young daughters until the next mating cycle begins. Then they persistently drive off their daughters to begin living on their own. The male cubs are driven off about three months earlier.

Scriptural Reference

Bears are mentioned thirteen times in scripture: *1 Samuel 17:34, 36, 37; 2 Samuel 7:8; 2 Kings 2:24; Proverbs 17:12; 28:15; Isaiah 11:7; 59:11; Lamentations 3:10; Daniel 7:5; Hosea 13:8; Revelation 13:2.*

Spiritual Application

As mentioned above, cubs spend a lot of time with their mothers compared to other animals. This is done to teach them all they need to know for their survival. This makes me think of the young man Timothy who had excellent training.

> *I am reminded of your sincere faith, a faith that dwelt first in your grandmother Lois and your mother Eunice and now, I am sure, dwells in you as well.* (2 Timothy 1:5)

We need people, preferably parents, to teach us how to make godly decisions and spiritually survive in this world. Timothy had such training. It started off when he was young and continued on through his life. Paul was introduced to him and referred to him as his son in the faith (*1 Timothy 1:2*). Timothy was ready to serve God because he was raised with that mind-set from his childhood.

Hebrew midwives had a custom that was used to stimulate nursing in a newborn. They would dip their finger in crushed dates and olive oil and rub it on the roof of the mouth of an infant to entice them to nurse. The term used for this process meant "create a desire."

God designed the family unit to teach and train children to be godly. Parents and grandparents should "create a desire" in their children to serve and follow after God. How can we do this? We lead by example. We live out our lives with the teachings of the Bible in our hearts so that it becomes part of our nature. Our children hear and see the scriptures daily lived out in front of them.

The mother bear prepares her cubs for life on their own by spending time with them, teaching them what they need to know. Lois and Eunice obviously spent time with Timothy, teaching and showing him how he should live. Shouldn't we be as concerned about teaching our own children how to walk in the ways of the Lord?

Train up a child in the ways he should go, and when he is old, he will not depart from it. (Proverbs 22:6)

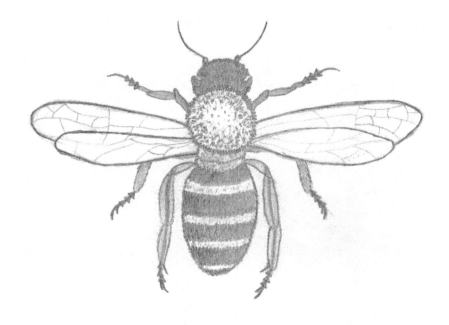

Bee (Apis mellifera)

Common Name: Honeybee

Background

One of the most remarkable creatures God created is the honeybee. When considering all the insects, it is the most studied and the most domesticated. The individual honeybee is reliant on the strength of the colony for survival. In a typical lifespan that only lasts six weeks, a single bee will produce one-twelfth of a teaspoon of honey. There are thousands of bees in a hive to perform all the jobs that need to be completed. It isn't uncommon during the peak of the floral bloom that a hive could have fifty thousand honeybees or more.

At an early age, I became fascinated with bees. I got my first package of Italians when I was fourteen. My intriguing curiosity has only grown over time. The more I learn about bees and beekeeping, the more I realize that I need to learn more. There are a few facts that the public knows about honeybees:

- They sting.
- They make honey.
- The queen is in charge.

It is much more complicated than that, but it is a good place to start.

Let's look a little deeper at this matriarchal structured system. Once the queen is successfully mated at a very young age, she is one of the very few creatures that predetermines the sex of each egg she will lay. A productive queen can lay as many as 1, 200 eggs a day. She performs a pre-laying inspection of the cell to get the needed information. It reminds me of the detailed inspection checklist a pilot goes through before taxiing the plane up to the tarmac. All the details seem unimportant to the passengers, but the pilot knows that the plane isn't going into the sky until a thorough check of all systems is accomplished.

Some of the things the queen does in her pre-laying inspection include the following:

- Check to make sure there is enough honey (carbohydrates) to feed the anticipated brood.
- Check to make sure there is enough pollen (protein) to feed the anticipated brood.
- Check to make sure the cell is clean and ready to receive an egg.
- Measure the width and depth of the cell.

Once she completes all these, she uses the information to lay either a fertile egg (female) or an infertile egg (male). The smaller cells are used to raise females or workers, and the larger cells will be used to raise males or drones.

Honeybees also exhibit something called floral constancy. This behavior provides information to the worker bees in such a way that she will let them know the location, color of the flower, and the flavor of the pollen or nectar she is to gather. Before this foraging bee leaves the colony, she has already been given all the information she needs from the scout. She will only collect pollen or nectar from one specific source. This makes honeybees crucial for plant pollination.

The scout returns to the colony and draws attention to itself by preforming the "waggle" dance. Foraging bees see these dancelike movements and decode them into coordinates to get the location of nectar or pollen. Once the scout gains the attention of the workers, she shares the flavor of the nectar or pollen. Here is an example of how it plays out. If the scout bee does the waggle dance to inform the foragers that there are apple trees in bloom 2.2 miles away in a northeastern direction, the foragers will take that information and make a "bee line" to those flowers on the apple trees. If there are peach, cherry, or plum trees in bloom, they will ignore all other flowers except for that which the scout has shared the information.

This floral constancy trait provides for a more efficient pollination of the specific plant in bloom. This will increase the overall fruit production of the source plant. It has been suggested that one out of every three bites of food we take is a direct result of bee pollination. This unique trait found in the honeybee accounts for as much as 80 percent of crop pollination in the United States.

Scriptural References

Bees are only found three times in all of scripture—*Deuteronomy 1:44*; *Judges 14:8*; and *Psalm 118:12*—whereas honey has fifty-three references and honeycomb has nine. See appendix 3 for a complete list of reference verses.

Spiritual Application

There are so many spiritual lessons we can learn from the honeybee that it would take up an entire book on its own. For now, let's continue with the thought process of floral constancy. It is vital for the health of the bees, plants, and all of creation. I see a likeness to that of our being called out for a specific purpose. God, in eternity past, knows me and has formed me and has prepared me to do great things on His behalf.

That foraging bee has been given all the information it needs to go and be productive for the greater good of the colony. If she deviates from her task, she harms the collective. If she gets sidetracked and fails to complete her task of gathering one-twelfth of a teaspoon of honey in her lifetime, will it really matter? Surely one of the other bees will step up and take up the slack.

We need to learn from one of the smallest creatures found in the Bible that the whole body suffers when one member does not do what God has created them to do. In *1 Corinthians 12:15* we see the effects Paul lays out if one part of the body does not function as it was designed. The entire body suffers. We need to have the desire to accomplish all that God has called us to do. Our purpose makes us unique in the work of God. But how do I know what things I am created to do? They are different for each of His workers. A single bee in the hive seems insignificant. Some may think that true of a single member of the body of Christ.

Ours is a unique task given by God that can be effectively carried out to completion if we use the tools provided by the Holy Spirit.

We are to go to the people God has prepared for us and "pollinate" them with the gospel message so that much fruit is produced. My individual flight path has been given to me. I shouldn't complain that it is too far or too hard of a journey. We shouldn't be envious of others because their path seems easier than our own. We are uniquely called and need to go where God has called us.

Flying off in your own direction will get you diverted, lost, and disconnected from the body. We are to stay focused on our own calling and the instructions we are given to complete our own task. We have been given a flight manual, the Bible, to guide us out to the fields that are ready for harvest. Let us purpose in our hearts to follow the path He has set before us.

As someone who manages an active apiary and teaches beekeeping courses, I have grown in my knowledge and appreciation of how much detail God has put into His creation. For whatever reason that pleased Him, God has placed so much complexity into this small, short-lived honeybee. How much more complex are we? Let's "bee" about our Father's business.

Behemoth (Apatosaurus)

Common Name: Brontosaurus

Background

This creature has been philosophically dissected and analyzed for years, but no one alive today can say just what it was with complete accuracy. Skeptics taunt that it is a mythological beast of great terror. Some scholars focus on the way the feet and muscles are described and reason it to be a hippopotamus. If we look at the full description, including things like the tail and its habitat, we have to evaluate it from all of the biblical information provided.

But first, we need to approach this creature as one that truly existed. For if we are like the skeptics, then we question the truthfulness of God's statements as it relates to this animal. If some pass judgment against it, questioning if it ever walked the planet, in essence, they are calling God a liar. That's not the direction we want to go.

From the text, we discover some things about Behemoth. This animal is an herbivore, meaning it eats plants. It has strong legs. Its bones resemble bronze columns, and its limbs are like iron. This animal is a big, strong plant eater. The text says it feeds on the mountains, in marshes, and in rivers. It goes where plant life flourishes, probably because it needs a lot of water and foliage to meet its nutritional needs.

Examining the known creatures from our present and past helps us narrow down the potential of what this could be. The Apatosaurus quickly comes to mind. Those around my age might say, "I never heard of that dinosaur before." Well, if I asked, "Do you know what a Brontosaurus is?" you would probably say, "Yes." It is the same creature, but the first discovery credit was changed, and it took on the newly ascribed name of Apatosaurus. This could easily fit all the descriptions we find in Job.

The Apatosaurus was the largest land animal known to exist. It could have reached as high as fifteen feet tall at the hips, ninety feet long, and could weigh over thirty tons. Being such a large herbivore, it would have to travel from the mountaintops to the marshes to fill its dietary requirements. The long neck would allow it to feed on treetops and on plant materials in swamps and water courses. It would require 1,500 gallons of water a day.

Scriptural Reference

This animal is only found in *Job 40:15*, but it takes ten verses to describe:

> *Behold Behemoth, which I made as I made you; he eats grass like an ox. Behold, his strength is in his loins, and his power is in the muscles of his belly. He makes his tail stiff like a cedar; the sinews of his thighs are knit together. His bones are tubes of bronze, his limbs like bars of iron. He is the first of the works of God; let Him who made him bring near His sword! For the mountains yield food for him where all the wild beast play. Under the lotus plants he lies, in the shelter of the reeds and in the marsh. For his shade the lotus trees cover him; the willows of the brook surround him. Behold if the river is turbulent he is not frightened; he is confident though Jordan rushes against his mouth. Can one take him by his eyes, or pierce his nose with a snare? (Job 40: 15–24)*

Spiritual Application

Why would God spend so much of His time (ten verses) describing a mythological beast to Job? In the last section of the book of Job, God gives a defense for how strong and powerful He is. He lays down a challenge to Job by asking, "Where were you when I did all this? Can you even come close to creating anything at all, let alone anything that compares to all the things I have created?"

In the verse shown above, God uses Behemoth as "exhibit A" in His defense and immediately states that it was one of His creatures. Just as sure as He made Job, He made Behemoth. God goes on to say that Behemoth is first of the works of God. Perhaps this suggests that on day six of creation, God created this creature first. Since God is a God of order, have you ever considered that God created the largest animals first all the way down to the smallest amoeba? Let me point out that creation was spoken into existence. It would have taken only seconds to create all living things. If we will be taken out of this world "in the twinkling of an eye" as we read in *1 Corinthians 15:52*, wouldn't it seem just as possible that He created the animals in the same manner?

As we "behold Behemoth," let us not give in to the other potential creatures that the world says it is. It isn't a terrifying mythical being to be feared. It doesn't eat people; it eats plants. The Apatosaurus is ten times larger than a hippopotamus. The hippo's tail isn't of any particularly impressive size, unless it was a mere seedling. And if it was just a cedar seedling, it would be bendable as opposed to being stiff. The hippo's natural habitat is in river bottoms, not on mountaintops.

One of Satan's most plentiful darts that he throws at us is doubt. I have a breaking story for you: evolution is "fake news." You cannot force two opposing viewpoints together and call it truth either. An older saying that still may be used today goes something like this, "God said it! I believe it! That settles it!" My believing God's word isn't the defining factor whether it is true. It should be changed to, "God said it! That settles it!" God explains the created world in Genesis. We cannot claim to be Christians, or "little Christs," and reject Genesis and the six days of creation. Those belief systems are the result of Satan's darts of doubt hitting us right on target. He has become such a marksman, it has weakened Christians all over the world.

Which takes more faith, to believe that our loving and all-powerful God made us and all the wondrous creatures in the world or that a thirty-ton Apatosaurus evolved from a single-celled accident of colliding molecules? I sure hope that your faith is in something much bigger than happenstance. I pray that your faith in the God of the Bible is as big as Behemoth.

> *I praise You for I am fearfully and wonderfully made. Wonderful are Your works, my soul knows it very well. (Psalm 139:14)*

Birds (Charadrius voceferus)

Common Name: Killdeer

Background

The world is filled with thousands of birds. They range in size from the small hummingbird to the very large ostrich. They each have amazing and unique traits. The tropical rainforest is filled with over four hundred types of colorful birds. North American is native to 914 bird species. In fact, you probably can spot many of them in your backyard or neighboring park. The easiest way to find out what species are native to your area is to hang out a bird feeder.

One of the resident birds that has always fascinated me is the killdeer. Most birds try to keep hidden and shy away from human contact. The killdeer draws attention to itself during the nesting period as a way to protect the eggs.

Killdeers are part of a larger grouping of ground-nesting birds that include the plovers. They nest on sandy beaches or stony open fields. Their nests are camouflaged well because their eggs look like small speckled rocks.

Because they nest on the ground, they keep constant watch against predators. Adult killdeers have a unique way to ward off potential threats from getting too close to their nest. They create a diversion by running away from the nesting location. If the would-be threat gets too close to the nest, the killdeer drops to the ground and fakes a broken wing.

These birds are masters at deception. Most of the time, the would-be attacker falls for the act and focuses on the "wounded" adult. When the theatrics work, the adult killdeer becomes the target and lures the threat further away. This process is repeated for as many times as it is needed until the predator loses interest. The killdeer should get an Oscar for their convincing performance. I personally have fallen victim to their alluring tactics.

Scriptural Reference

Although there are nearly thirty different types of birds listed in the Bible, the general term "bird(s)" is found fifty-one times. The most common phrase is "birds of the air," which is used twenty-one times.

Spiritual Application

When David was on the run from Saul, he often felt he had a predator chasing after him. On one of those occasions while King David was being pursued, his journeys took him to Gath. A servant of King Achish recognized David, and taunting remarks made it clear that David was going to be held captive to be delivered to Saul. No doubt, Saul had a bounty on David's head.

1 Samuel 21:13 says, "*So he disguised his sanity before them, and acted insanely in their hands, and scribbled on the doors of the gates, and let his saliva run down into his beard.*"

David created a diversion using theatrics to make King Achish think he was a madman. David faked insanity to get out of a potential life-threatening situation. Saul had connections with many other kings and would have compensated anyone handsomely if they delivered David to him. His performance must have been equal to that of the killdeer. They both avoided trouble by "playacting."

It was in this time in David's life that he writes Psalm 34. This powerful Psalm reminds us how God delivers His own out of dangerous situations. It comforts those who are anxious, are fearful, and need encouragement. Here, David penned the words while on the run because of the death threat Saul had placed on his head. From his writings, it is unmistakable.

David found comfort in knowing God was in control and protecting him through the trial.

I sought the Lord and He answered me,
And He delivered me from all my fears,
They looked to Him and were radiant,
And their faces shall never be ashamed.
This poor man cried and the Lord heard him,
And saved him out of all his troubles,
The angel of the Lord encamps around those that fear Him,
And rescues them,
Oh taste and see that the Lord is good.
How blessed is the man who takes refuge in Him! (Psalm 34:4–8)

Bittern (Botarus lentiginosus)

Common Name: American Bittern

Background

The bittern is part of a group of birds that are found in shallow water wading habitats. Their long necks and long spike-like bills are used to catch small fish. Bitterns have some of the most interesting common names. In some parts of the country they are commonly called stake drivers, pumperlunks, and bog bulls. These reclusive waterbirds live among the reeds and rushes and are usually spotted standing with their head and bill pointed upward. By holding itself "at attention," its dark earth-tone lines allow it to blend in with the surrounding hydrophytic vegetation. The unique sound made by the males during mating helps us understand how some of these common names came about. The call resembles the sound of a wooden stake being driven into the wet ground. The bittern accomplishes this by swallowing large amounts of air and convulsively pulsing the air out by jerking its body. This distinct sound can travel nearly a mile.

Scriptural Reference

The bittern is referred to three times in two Old Testament books, *Isaiah 14:23, 34:11* and *Zephaniah 2:14.*

Spiritual Application

Each time the bittern is mentioned, it is in context with judgment from the Lord. The places and nations being judged and then destroyed will no longer be a dwelling place for people to live. The bittern takes up residence in areas away from human disturbance and utilizes these marshy areas quite effectively. The bittern pounds out his solemn, rhythmic dirge as if to mourn all those that fall under God's judgment. *Ezekiel 20:35–38* gives us the events leading up to Israel's judgment:

> *And I will bring you into the wilderness of the people, and there will I plead with you face to face. Like as I pleaded with your fathers in the wilderness of the land of Egypt, so will I plead with you, saith the Lord God. And I will cause you to pass under the rod, and I will bring you into the bond of the covenant; and I will purge out from among you the rebels, and them that transgress against me! I will bring them forth, out of the country where they sojourn, and they shall not enter into the land of Israel: and Ye shall know that I am the Lord.*

Salvation always comes down to having a personal relationship with the Lord. Without it, your eternity is destined for a place far worse than the solitude of the bittern's home. Your final resting place will be a place of judgment. A place of no rest. A place where the fire is not quenched and the worm never dies. Wouldn't it be far better to call upon the name of the Lord today for salvation and begin your personal relationship with Him right now?

Cattle (Bos taurus)

Common Name: Angus Cattle

Background

Growing up on a farm teaches you a lot about animal behavior. I remember at a very young age having the chore of bringing the milk cows in from afternoon pasture for the evening milking. Most of the time they were just as interested in getting to the barn as I was. But every once in a while, there was a cow that was headstrong and wanted to go in a different direction. I guess that's why fences were invented. When constructed properly, fences do a good job of containing most of the animals. Those few problematic cows just seem to go in the direction their head is pointing.

There is a science to properly handling cattle. One of the foremost experts is Temple Grandin. In a time when the cattle industry was dominated by men, Temple Grandin broke out of her autistic shell and changed the way cattle handling facilities are designed. She now teaches and gives lectures on animal behavior and holds a doctorate degree. I've had the pleasure of meeting her and sitting in on several of her lectures. She stresses the important and proper use of fencing to control cattle.

Most farm kids learn at an early age how to build and maintain fences. Cattle like to know where their boundaries are, and as Dr. Grandin discovered, they like to move in circular patterns. Fences serve two primary functions:

1. Protect cattle from danger.
2. Keep cattle contained.

Life outside the fence can be a very dangerous place. Therefore, fences are used to help manage the herd. They give the cattle boundaries. Only the rebellious cows challenge the fences. They are the ones that seem to think the grass is always greener on the other side.

Many local units of government have precepts, or written laws, requiring livestock owners to safely contain their animals on their property. Cattle roaming freely can be a safety issue for both them and others. Well-maintained fences address the above-mentioned primary functions.

Scriptural Reference

There are many names that fall under the bovine category. Here is what we find in the Scriptures:

- "Bull(s)" found 12 times.
- "Bullock" found 137 times.
- "Calf" or "calves" found 48 times.
- "Cattle" found 149 times.
- "Heifer(s)" found only 2 times.
- "Ox" or "oxen" found 153 times.

See the complete list of references found in appendix 3.

Spiritual Application

In plain and simple terms, the Bible is the fence for believers. It establishes the boundaries of life from God's point of view. Spiritual guidelines serve two primary functions:

1. Protect believers from danger.
2. Keep believers contained.

How does it keep us from danger? The laws, statutes, and precepts are given to us through the Word of God.

Teach me, oh Lord, the way of Your statutes, and I shall keep it until the end. Give me understanding, and I shall keep Your law; Indeed, I shall observe it with my whole heart. Make me walk in the path of Your commandments, for I delight in it. Incline my heart to Your testimonies, and not to covetousness. Turn away my eyes from looking at worthless things; and revive me in Your way. Establish Your word to your servant, who is devoted to fearing You. Turn away my reproach which I dread, for Your judgments are good. Behold, I long for Your precepts; Revive me in Your righteousness. (Psalm 119:33–40)

When we stray outside the established boundaries, we invite danger to creep in. Satan gives us a false sense of how great it is living outside the rules. He even weakens the barriers by compromise to make it seem easier to follow the direction our head is pointing us toward. Lot found this out as soon as he pitched his tent toward Sodom (*Genesis 13:18*).

Our head contains all five of the sensory systems in our body, and they can certainly lead us astray. Our spiritual fence lines get cut, gates are left open, and storms come with the power to knock our fences down. The outside looks easy and safe to traverse. We think we can linger along the fence lines and jump back across to safety if things get tough. Usually the danger doesn't happen right along the fence lines. You keep building up false self-confidence and wander further from the boundaries. When danger comes, the safe harbor of the fence is out of sight. It is alluring on the edge of the boundaries. That is how most people get drawn further away.

We need to be like the Psalmist and "delight in Your commandments" and "observe it with my whole heart." If we should stray outside the boundaries God has laid out for us, there is a way back into the fold. *1 John 1:9* says, "*If we confess our sins, He is faithful and just to forgive us our sins and to cleanse us from all unrighteousness.*" Our desire ought to be to please God with our whole heart. To do that, we need to know and follow the boundaries spelled out in God's Holy Word.

I've heard that people write the following quote in the inside cover of their Bible as a reminder of how we should live: "This book [the Bible] will keep you from sin; or sin will keep you from this book." Now that's solid advice to live by.

"Any glimpse into the life of an animal quickens our own and makes it so much the larger and better in every way."

John Muir

Chameleon
(Anoles carolinensis)

Common Name: American Chameleon

Background

The chameleon is a lizard or anole that can change the color of his skin. The American chameleon can present colors from light green to brown. These color changes allow them to camouflage themselves from would-be predators. These color changes are also used to send social messages to other chameleons. For those of you over the age of fifty, think of them as natural mood rings. For those under fifty, you might have to research them. The color changes are instant messaging for mating or guarding their territory.

This unique trait is accomplished by changing the distance between guanine crystals found under the skin. Rearranging the spacing changes the wavelength of the reflected light that penetrates the skin and bounces off the crystals. Even though they have a natural hue, how can we tell what their real color is supposed to be if they are changing it all of the time? We can assume that when they are calm and do not feel threatened, their true colors are exposed.

Scriptural Reference

The chameleon is only found once in scripture, *Leviticus 11:30.* Here it is listed among the unclean animals that creep upon the earth. Reptiles are all considered unclean.

Spiritual Application

What if you had the ability to blend in with your surroundings and camouflage your true colors? People can infiltrate other groups of people and pretend to be someone they are not. Normally we would call these people spies or moles. Their true colors are hidden to gain advantage or collect some important information.

One man in scripture fits the description quite well. His name is Haman from the book of Esther. Haman displays his territorial colors every time he sets his eyes upon Mordecai. Haman feels he deserves to have the king's top position. Haman also harbors hatred toward the entire Jewish people. In the following passage, we see a lot of "colors" coming from Haman, but his true colors present themselves at the end of the passage.

> *And Haman went out that day joyful and glad of heart. But when Haman saw Mordecai in the king's gate, that he neither rose nor trembled before him, he was filled with wrath against Mordecai. Nevertheless, Haman restrained himself and went home and sent and brought his friends and his wife Zeresh. And Haman recounted to them the splendor of his riches, the number of his sons, all the promotions with which the king had honored him, and how he had advanced him above the officials and servants of the king. Then Haman said, "Even Queen Esther let no one but me come with the king to the feast she prepared. And tomorrow also I am invited by her together with the king. Yet all of this is worth nothing to me, so long as I see Mordecai the Jew sitting at the king's gate." Then his wife Zeresh and all his friends said to him, "Let a gallows 50 cubits high be made, and in the morning, tell the king to have Mordecai hanged upon it. Then go joyfully with the king to the feast." The idea pleased Haman, and he had the gallows made. (Esther 5:9–14)*

Haman camouflaged his true feelings for Mordecai when he saw him at the king's gate. It was a privileged place reserved for those who held the king's favor. He only let his true colors show in front of his wife and close friends. He called Mordecai a Jew, which was used to show disrespect to the Jewish people. But in the end, Haman's true colors were seen by everyone in the kingdom when the very same gallows he gave the orders to build for Mordecai would be used on him. In a strange twist of fate, when the king found out Haman's true colors, justice was served.

What are your true colors? What are the hidden intentions that drive you to do the things you do? God knows your heart and knows your true colors. They can't be hidden from Him. Like guanine crystals under the chameleon's skin, we need to move the hidden agendas around so that when the light of God hits us, the wavelength reflects our true colors. The colors that display the love of God in us.

Deer (*Odocoileus virginianus*)

Common Name: White-Tailed Deer

Background

As fall approaches in North American, many people set their goal on hunting and bagging a trophy buck. The excitement of the hunt is only bested when the tag is filled with an animal that you can put in your freezer and hang on the wall. There is a lot of serious money spent by hunters every year in this pursuit. It's not just the hunters that relish a massive set of antlers. The deer themselves find glory in what is adorned on their head.

Male white-tailed deer grow a new set of antlers every year. Not every buck can merit a high-yielding score on the Boone and Crockett or Pope and Young ranking systems. There are two basic things that determine the size of the antlers:

1. Heredity: The number of points a deer will have is more of a function of its DNA than anything else. If genetically they are predisposed to be an eight-point, that is generally what they will be for most of their lives. In captivity, a buck could live out its life for twelve years, and eight of those twelve years it had eight points. Some deviation occurred during its early years and later years, but often, the basic shape and number of points didn't deviate much.

2. Nutrition: Food and mineral intake can greatly affect the diameter and height of the antlers. A mineral block will not

grow more points, but it will help to make more mass. Ample amounts of quality forage availability can be a factor as well.

Male white-tails annually shed their antlers. Studies have shown that males (bucks) are not able to breed females (does) if they have shed their antlers. This narrows down the breeding season, or "rut," in the fall. The shortening of daylight hours, coupled with the hormones racing through the male's body, forces it to focus solely on mating. They have been known to act crazy during this period.

The bucks take pride in the crown of calcium and minerals they display on their heads. He will fight off other males for breeding rights and defend his territory, which can be about one square mile. But come January, the antlers fall to the ground and are left to become food sources for rodents in the wild. This pride of having a huge rack is quickly gone, and he blends in with all the other deer in the woods. It's almost as if he is stripped of his massive horns and becomes just another deer.

Scriptural Reference

Several different names are used for members of the cervidae family that can be grouped into deer. The Bible uses these terms:

- "Deer" used once in *Deuteronomy 12:5.*
- "Fallow deer" used once in *1 Kings 4:23.*
- "Hart(s)" occurs eleven times.
- "Roebuck" or "roe(s)" shows up seventeen times.

See appendix 3 for a complete list of reference verses.

Spiritual Application

Man, like the buck with a full set of antlers, is prideful. We adorn ourselves with outward embellishments to draw attention to ourselves. People like being the center of attention and having their moment of glory. This prideful thinking goes to their heads, and they let the outward define them, only to find out that the outward man is fleeting and the adornment doesn't last.

Even in our spiritual lives, we will be rewarded with crowns if we follow biblical commands and run our race well. But this too doesn't last for all of eternity. In fact, it doesn't last very long at all. For when we receive our crowns, we will realize that it isn't because of anything in and of ourselves. The crowns are because Jesus Christ was living in and through us. What are we to do with these marvelous rewards we get in eternity? We will take our lead from the twenty-four elders.

Revelation 4:10–11 says, "*The four and twenty elders fall down before Him that sat on the throne, and worship Him that liveth for ever and ever, and cast their crowns before the throne, saying, Thou art worthy, O Lord, to receive glory and honor and power: for thou hast created all things, and for thy pleasure they are and were created.*"

Our Boone and Crockett or Pope and Young wall mounts, our Purple Hearts, our blue ribbons, or our bowling trophies won't mean a thing once we see Jesus face-to-face. Everything we have with lasting value has already been given to us in Christ.

Dog (Canis lupus)

Common Name: Dog

Background

According to the world canine organization, there are 332 breeds of dogs. The smallest dog on record was only 1.4 pounds, while the largest, a mastiff, weighed in at 382 pounds. Dogs come in a variety of sizes, shapes, and colors. Because of their different characteristic traits, dogs have been trained for specific purposes. Some can sniff out explosives, and others find cancer in a person. Some make good guards to protect your property, while others make good guides to help those without sight. They can hunt, pull sleds, swim, or provide comfort to humans. It is no wonder the world refers to them as "man's best friend."

I only remember one fifteen-month period in my life when I didn't have a dog. Growing up on a farm meant that dogs were always around. Some dogs were used for hunting, some for herding cattle, but most were just for pleasure. I've heard my dad say from time to time that eventually, one of his dogs would outlive him.

Mankind has become very attached to our furry four-footed companions. Personally, I prefer large dogs. The bigger the better. Of the numerous breeds of large dogs, the golden retriever is my favorite. Retrievers have breed characteristics that give them a great personality. Their characteristic traits include friendly, confident, intelligent, trustworthy, and devoted. The average golden retriever has a twelve-year life span.

Scriptural Reference

"Dog," "dog's," or "dogs" is found forty-one times in the Bible. Most occurrences are in the Old Testament. Of all the references, the only one that sheds any sort of positive light on their character traits is found in *Job 30:1*. Here, the verse hints of having dogs keep watch over the flocks in the field. In the context, however, the main thought of the passage is presented as a disgrace.

Spiritual Application

Did the writers of the Bible get this one wrong? What we read in scripture doesn't match up with what the worldview says about dogs today. Almost all the passages paint a less-than-favorable picture of dogs as they relate to mankind. If we were to only use what is found in scripture to define the nature of dogs, their character traits would include unclean, evil, and scavengers. Dogs were used as a derogatory term for non-Jewish (Gentile) or the unsaved.

Dogs in the Bible parallel an unregenerate man. One of the more graphic depictions is found in the demise of a wicked queen, Jezebel, where the dogs consume her flesh in *1 Kings 21:23* and *2 Kings 9:10, 36*.

Many verses on dogs deal with their tongue or their eating habits. In *Judges 7:5*, Gideon's men are judged based on how they drink water from a stream. Those that lapped up the water with their tongues like dogs were not selected. In *Psalm 26:11* and *2 Peter 2:22* we find the writers focusing on one of a dog's more disgusting trait of returning to their own vomit.

The biblical traits of the dog are opposite of the character traits of the golden retriever. What has changed? Why has the world's opinion turned 180 degrees from the biblical perception of dogs? Let's look at two perspectives on answering these questions.

Firstly, the worldview on any subject is always going to come up short when measured against God's word. Dogs, no matter how much we have domesticated them over the thousand or so years, are still dogs. If left undomesticated, they would revert to the wild creatures that they were. Those dogs that go feral have no fear of humans and are even more of a threat than their cousins, the wolves.

Secondly, and probably more importantly, dogs represented Gentiles in the Jewish culture. Gentiles were unclean half-breeds that were not accepted as part of God's chosen nation, Israel. But the good news is that Christ came to seek and save that which was lost or not accepted. His mission wasn't to only save the nation of Israel. His mission was to reconcile all people unto Himself. Because of Christ's salvation work on the cross, the Gentile has equal access to God the Father through His Son. *Romans 3:10* says, "*None is righteous, no not one,*" because "we are all as an unclean thing and our righteousnesses are as filthy rags" (*Isaiah 64:6*).

We have inherited our sin nature by birth. Our root character traits fall way short of what God requires to be considered good. But when we put on the character traits of Jesus Christ, all of our character flaws are overlooked because God sees us as having Christ's righteousness.

So the biblical writers did not get it wrong. Dogs will always be dogs. But they can be domesticated and can change into something more desirable and good. But let's not put too much emphasis in the world's statement that the dog is man's best friend. Jesus Christ will always be man's best friend. He came as a man to redeem mankind, and that makes Him the best friend we will ever know!

2 Corinthians 5:17 says, "*Therefore, if any man be in Christ, he is a new creature: old things are passed away; behold all things are becoming new.*"

Eagle
(*Haliaeetus leucocephalus*)

Common Name: Bald Eagle

Background

Many would agree that one of God's most majestic creatures on the earth is the eagle. This powerful bird of prey can fly at high altitudes and soar for hours on its average six-foot-wide wing span. This raptor, with all its strength, was placed on the endangered species list in 1972. But because of improved habitat and conservation efforts, it has made a serious comeback and was removed from the endangered list in 2007. People have become so fascinated with eagles that they spend hours watching live feeds from cameras to observe these birds building nests, laying eggs, hatching their young, caring for them, and eventually leaving the nest.

Eagle feathers are magnificent and are held in high esteem for Native American ceremonies. In fact, very few people (Native Americans and falconers) are granted permission to have eagle feathers in their possession. If someone is caught having them without the legal authority and proper permits, they can be fined, imprisoned, or both.

The feather is of great value to the eagle as well. A broken, damaged, or missing feather can mean the difference between catching its prey and just missing it. Too many missed meals can lead to a weakened bird where the hunter becomes the hunted. The necessary process of systematically replacing each feather is called molting. All birds go through a molting process, but it varies between the different species. Eagles and other soaring birds must go through this to keep their wings strong to hunt for food. The process isn't painful, but it can put the birds at a disadvantage. When completed, the eagle is stronger and has better control over flight. New feathers replace old, weakened, battered ones.

This molting process isn't some random loss of feathers. On the contrary, it is a complex, synchronized procedure. Feathers are replaced on opposite wings at the same location. The eagle would not be able to survive a random loss of feathers. Let's examine the what-ifs.

What if all the feathers came out at the same time? The eagle would not be able to fly. This means it would not be able to properly regulate its body temperature and could go into hypothermia. Feathers provide insulation for the bird in harsher climates. Otherwise, the bird would surely die.

What if the feathers came out from only one side at a time? The eagle might be capable of flying, but only in an uncontrollable circle. The eagle would have to be already in the air to realize the problem, and by then it would be too late. The result would be a crash landing. Follow this regression example:

- Uncontrollable flight leads to a crash landing.
- Too many crash landings lead to broken bones.
- Too many broken bones lead to a broken spirit.
- A broken spirit reduces the chance that the eagle will ever fly again. It is still an eagle, but it isn't functioning as designed by God.

When a master falconer (someone who has been properly trained by a mentor and has legal permission to keep birds of prey) sees a feather that is broken or damaged, they repair it by a method called imping. Imping is taking a shed feather that has been saved to replace the broken or damaged one. Imping restores balance to the eagle's wings and, therefore, helps it to regain flight control.

Scriptural References

The Bible has thirty-four references that include eagles. Probably the most familiar one is found in *Isaiah 40:31*, "*They shall mount up with wings like eagles.*" See appendix 3 for a complete list of reference verses.

Spiritual Application

When it comes right down to it, we are worse off than eagles. We have an inherent nature within us to crash-land and damage ourselves. We really don't have control over our life, and we break ourselves up. If we do this too many times, we might lose the desire to fly again. We think we are in control, but like the example of the eagle that has molted only on one side, by the time we figure out the problem, it is too late, and down we go. Other times we are carried off by winds of improper doctrines and find it difficult to make it back. Like the eagle with the broken or damaged feathers, we become unbalanced.

The only one that sets things right is the Master, Jesus Christ. *2 Corinthians 5:21* (NKJ) says, "*For He made Him who knew no sin to be sin for us, that we might become the righteousness of God in Him.*" Our beloved mentor, Jesus Christ, took our brokenness upon Himself while we were being carried off by strange winds. He gave that which was needed for us, His very life, so that we might have life. He brings balance, structure, and order to our chaotic, out-of-control lives.

The imping procedure that the master falconer does to repair the broken feathers is certainly not deserved. However, the kindness of the caregiver restores and repairs the damaged parts. What Christ did for us can be called imping too. We lengthen the word out and call it imputing. He imputed His righteousness on us, and we are called His children. His truths are so amazing that *All Nature Sings* the praises of His marvelous gifts.

"A good man is concerned for the welfare of his animals." Proverbs 12:10

Flocks and Herds

Common Name: Barnyard Animals

Background

The family farm I grew up on always had a wide variety of animals. The multi-species included chickens, geese, rabbits, goats, sheep, beef and dairy cattle, ponies, horses, and numerous cats and dogs. The noisiest time of the day was feeding time. From outside of the barn, it would sound chaotic because the humans were trying to get all their chores completed as quickly as possible. The problem was each group of animals wanted to be fed first. Their impatience translated into commotion.

The farm was a gathering place for family and friends. Growing up with all sorts of animals gave me insight of their basic behavior patterns. Cattle especially seemed to know when strangers were around. The other animals sensed it too. Noises, reactions, and movements became accelerated when something or someone new was added to the daily routine.

Probably the loudest thing on the farm wasn't an animal at all. It was the vacuum pump that could be heard twice every day. When it was running, animals and humans alike knew it was milking time. The animals all seemed to settle down as the humans taking care of them did the milking. This was the most important part of the morning and evening because the bulk of the farm income came in the form of the monthly milk check. Consequently, my grandfather didn't tolerate much commotion during milking time.

After the last cow was milked and the equipment washed and hung on the rack to dry, the other farm activities would be tended to. One of those jobs I remember doing was sweeping out the mangers. These were concrete feed bunkers aligned in front of the dairy stanchions.

Scriptural Reference

Groups of domesticated livestock either out in pasture or in stalls are commonly found in scripture. The term "flock" or "flocks" is used 187 times. The term "herd" or "herds" is used 55 times. Most of the time these are found in the Old Testament, but a few times they are mentioned in the New Testament. See appendix 3 for a complete list of reference verses.

Spiritual Application

One such use of a gathering of multi-species of animals was in a stable in Bethlehem just over two thousand years ago. We all should be familiar with the Nativity and the place of Christ's birth. The timing of His birth happened as travelers adhered to the decree that was sent out by Caesar Augustus requiring everyone to return to their place of birth to be counted and appropriately taxed. This can be found in *Luke 2:1*. The inn that normally would be available was already filled. Mary and Joseph were offered shelter in the stable. This would have been the barn of their period.

Most people have this image of the stable as a quiet little shelter, a clean, private, peaceful place. It probably was a rather noisy, dirty enclosure filled with animals owned by the innkeeper and by those occupying the inn. From my own experience of growing up on a farm, the combination of unfamiliar people and animals spending the night together would be anything but quiet and peaceful. Now we need to add the labor and delivery of a baby. This certainly would have created a lot of noise and commotion.

The hymn "Away in a Manger" says in the second verse, "*No crying He makes.*" If the song lyrics are correct, amidst all that was going on that very special night, the baby Jesus was at peace. We need to understand that the other occupants of the stable were probably not. This reminds me of a time some thirty years later when Jesus and His disciples were in a boat on a lake when a violent storm came upon them. The disciples were frantic and feared for their lives. And where was Jesus during this treacherous storm? He was sleeping peacefully in the stern of the ship (*Mark 4:35–42*).

These two incidents give us insight of one of the names of Jesus, the Prince of Peace. Throughout His humanity, He is characterized as a man of peace. It doesn't matter what chaos the world is experiencing; our Lord is in control.

While studying this portion of scripture, I discovered something interesting about the audience at Jesus's birth. Before the shepherds, the wise men, or the innkeeper saw the Christ child, those noisy barnyard animals were among the first to see Him. Why is this something worth considering? They are just simple animals. They have no understanding or need for a Savior. They don't have an eternal soul. Yet for several thousand years under the priestly system, animals were the substituted sacrifices that provided a temporary covering for man's sin.

Now, the only One worthy to provide an eternal sacrifice had come. "*Emmanuel, God with us*" was here. The Savior of mankind became flesh and dwelt among us. He was the complete, acceptable, and perfect sacrifice. No longer would animals have to be killed to cover man's sins.

> *Behold the Lamb of God that takes away the sins of the world.* (*John 1:29*)

This sense of justice and compassion for the domesticated animals that previously were the means for man's temporary atonement of sin, Christ's birth and eventual death meant that animals no longer had to die. Those animals in the stable didn't have the ability to understand who that baby was or how He would change the world forever. Nor did they understand that the child was God in the flesh, the very One who created all things. He was the

One who cared enough to share His birth with them in the stable. Ultimately, He shared it with all of mankind. And because of that, all of creation should be thankful. The words of an old hymn written by William Newell seems to capture the depth of thankfulness we all should realize:

> *Oh, the love that drew salvation's plan!*
> *Oh, the grace that brought it down to man!*
> *Oh, the mighty gulf that God did span at Calvary!*

Giraffe
(Giraffa camelopardalis)

Common Name: Giraffe

Background

When a new giraffe is born in the wild, it happens with the mother or cow in a standing position. So the very first experience the baby giraffe or calf has is falling eight feet to the ground. To further add insult to injury, it usually lands on its back. What a rough start! It shakes its head to clear away the embryonic fluids from the eyes, ears, and mouth. The next chore is to stand up.

Now the cow straddles over the newborn, and instead of instinctively licking and cleaning it off, she kicks it. I am sure this isn't what you or the calf would expect. This is done to motivate the calf into standing up on all four feet. Once the baby can get up, you would think the mother would allow it to nurse to get that much-needed colostrum into their system. But instead, the cow head-butts the calf back to the ground. This process is repeated, over and over again.

What a harsh welcome into the world! But in the jungle, it is a harsh environment. The weak and young are first to fall victim to those seeking to fill their own bellies. The jungle is filled with lions, hyenas, vultures, cheetahs, and more that are looking for an easy meal. A newborn giraffe weighing in at 150 pounds would suit just fine.

Being able to get up fast and be in a full-out run in a split second is essential for survival. It is more important than your first meal.

The mother giraffe knows this, and although we think it is cruel, it is a necessity for the calf. Otherwise, it will be consumed.

Scriptural Reference

There are no references to giraffes in the Bible. Why would I write a book on animals in the Bible and include something that isn't there? The title of my book is *All Nature Sings*. Even if an animal isn't found in the pages of scripture, we still have the witness of creation that points us to an almighty Creator (*Romans 1:19–20*).

Spiritual Application

Have you ever had a time in your life when it seemed like, no matter what, you were constantly being knocked down? For me that was middle school. I was a middle child in middle school, and to make matters worse, I was one of the shortest boys in my class. I felt unsure of myself, and the other kids capitalize on it. They were relentless. If you had any sort of flaw, it was pointed out, and you were ridiculed.

Joseph in the Bible had about as rough of start as anyone. He was the eleventh boy out of twelve, and his father made it clear that he was his favorite son. That didn't sit too well with the ten brothers ahead of him. Joseph was verbally abused, thrown into a well, sold into slavery, falsely accused, and then forgotten in prison.

Joseph, like the young giraffe, couldn't catch a break. All this would have given Joseph ample cause to resent God and walk away from Him. However, all this was done to place Joseph in the exact position he needed to be in to save his entire family and many others from a deadly drought and famine.

Genesis 50:20 says, "*As for you, you meant evil against me, but God meant it for good, to bring it about that many people should be kept alive, as they are today.*"

Most of the time we cringe when we suffer verbal, physical, financial, or emotional abuse. We become withdrawn and bitter and are not willing to see beyond our own despair. Yet God is still in control. He is still on His throne. And even during the rough patches we go through, He has it all planned out to be a benefit to Him and others in the end.

When life head-butts you, just remember that God is setting you up to be a blessing to others somewhere down the road. Job had everything except his life taken away from him, and he remained faithful. God gave him the ability to struggle through the attacks as an example to the rest of humanity. Like the tough love of the mother giraffe who knows what is best for her calf, God allows trials to come our way. He has our best interest in mind. He gives us His solemn promise that He will never leave us or forsakes us (*Hebrews 13:5*).

Note: The information on the way the newborn giraffe is taught was presented during a radio broadcast that I listened to while driving on a trip, and I didn't get the name of the broadcast and radio station to give proper credit to the speaker. The speaker spoke with a British accent.

Gnat
(Drosophila melanogaster)

Common Name: Fruit Fly

Background

One of the smallest creatures listed in the Bible is the gnat. The term "gnat" can apply to several different species. The most common species is perhaps the fruit fly. They have been used for scientific study and research in genetics because they are easily raised, they reproduce quickly, and they are short-lived. Their average life span is thirty days, depending on the temperature. The adult only lives about two weeks.

For the very same reasons that scientists like gnats, most everybody else despises them and thinks of them as pests. Eggs are laid on fruit and usually enter our homes as unhatched larvae. Once they get into your kitchen, it is a battle getting rid of them. Isn't it amazing how something so small and with such a short lifespan can still cause us a great deal of frustration?

Scriptural References

The gnat is only found in one verse, *Matthew 23:24.* In context, it shows how we obsess on the smallest of things and don't even consider the obvious.

Spiritual Application

We, like the gnat, only live a short time on this world. King Solomon pursued wisdom only to find in the end that all is vanity as found in *Ecclesiastes 1:14*.

In the New Testament, we see that life is fleeting. *James 4:14* says, "*Yet you do not know what tomorrow will bring. What is your life? For you are a mist that appears for a little time and then vanishes.*"

Even if we live to be one hundred, compared to all of eternity, it is nothing. From the day we are born until we die, we have only a short time here on planet Earth. We need to be motivated to make every moment count. We only have a set number of days.

A co-worker once added up all the holidays, vacation days, sick days, personal days, weekends, and in-climate weather days he had available. Added on to that are coffee breaks, lunch breaks, water-cooler talk, and general idle time at work. He came up with a shockingly small number of days in a given year that could actually be counted as true work.

Our life is like that too. If we take the time to figure out how much of our day is spent doing what God expects us to do, it isn't much. How precious few the days we really have. Our days are numbered!

We are told in *Psalm 90:12*, "*So teach us to number our days that we may get a heart of wisdom.*" God, help us to recognize how brief our life is. Help us to understand that how we spend our time is important. The small gnat has that figured out. Why can't we? When we fully perceive that we are only here for a moment in time, it should motivate us to fill each day with making a difference for eternity.

Teach us to count the days
Teach us to make the days count
Lead us in better ways
Somehow our souls forgot
Life means so much.
Every day is a gift you've been given.
Make the most of your time every minute you're living.
(Chris Rice, "Life Means So Much")

Hawk (Buteo jamaicensus)

Common Name: Red-Tailed Hawk

Background

The red-tail is the most common of the hawk species found in North America. It is well adapted to live in forested or open areas but can be found in cities and deserts. They are the easiest birds of prey to identify because they have pronounced red tail feathers as viewed from above. They are part of the soaring hawks. When the sunlight shines down on the rocks, water, and soil, some of the heat is reflected. This creates heat thermals or currents of vertical air that generate lift for the birds. These soaring hawks are captivating to watch as they glide for long periods of time without flapping their wings.

Red-tails will migrate to warmer southern climates in the fall. One winter while driving in the south, I saw red-tails lined up like mile markers along Interstate 40, scoping the grassy strips along the road for rabbits and mice. I was heading to Arkansas for a four-month college internship. I guess you could say I was doing a little soaring of my own.

Scriptural Reference

"Hawk" is used five times in scripture, and all references are found in the Old Testament. They are found in *Leviticus 11:16* (twice); *Deuteronomy 14:15* (twice); and *Job 39:26*, where it says, "*It is by Your understanding that the hawk soars and spreads his wings toward the earth.*"

Spiritual Application

Catching heat thermals for the soaring hawks appear effortless for the birds. I am certain it takes a lot of practice and concentration to learn how to harvest the power of these updrafts. Each wing must be stretched out and held in position for a long time. I have watched these birds ride those thermals until they were nothing but a speck in the sky.

The soaring hawks remind me of God's peculiar way of helping Moses in Exodus 17, where he led the captive Israelite's out of Egypt to be God's chosen nation in a new land. While they were working their way toward the Promised Land, we learn that they are confronted by the Amalekites. God told Moses that they would be victorious in battle if he held his staff over his head. I am sure it was easy at first, but as the day lingered on, Moses grew fatigued, and his ability to hold the staff as directed weakened. Aaron and Hur came alongside of Moses and lifted each arm when he grew weary. Moses kept his staff raised until sundown, and the Amalekites were defeated.

Sometimes living out the Christian life can be spiritually, physically, and emotionally tiring. You just can't keep going on your own strength. It is during those times that God sends other Christian believers your way to help hold you up and encourage you. Christians often get wounded or grow weary in the battle and need help. We can't continually hold our staff over our heads. God never intended for us to do it alone. Moses was given help by those closest to him.

Nothing uplifts a person more than receiving help in a time of need. Sometimes it comes by a visit or a phone call from a friend that lifts your spirits. And sometimes it comes from a complete stranger. However, nothing matches the sense of relief when God Himself is the one that does the lifting. There is no greater assurance for a believer than when God comes and backs you up.

When the red-tailed hawk soars, it looks effortless as they circle for hours. But it is the rising heat thermals providing the lift. You cannot see them, but they are there carrying the hawk to new heights. God provides the power through the Holy Spirit to make living the Christian life look effortless. He gives us the spiritual, physical, and emotional strength we need to live a victorious life. We don't see Him, but the evidence of His presence is all around us, lifting us up.

> *Let us then with confidence draw near to the throne of grace, that we may receive mercy and grace to help in a time of need. (Hebrews 4:16)*

Horse (Equine caballus)

Common Name: Horse, Draft Horse

Background

There are countless benefits for having been raised on a farm. The small dairy herd, crop fields, pastures, woods, and large garden had "hard work" written all over them. Still, I wouldn't trade that experience for the world. Every square foot of the farm and the buildings had a purpose. Long after tractors replaced the draft horses to reduce the time to get things done, my grandfather chose to keep them around. He had a designated pasture just for the horses. The cows and crops paid the bills, but the horses provided pleasure and were a link back to his younger days.

Horses used to be the backbone of how most work got accomplished. They pulled the equipment that plowed, planted, and harvested the crops, and provided the means of transportation. Draft horses worked hard and needed to be fed well to stay fit and healthy for the next day's work. They worked hard six days a week and usually got to rest on Sunday. This was a day of rest for man and beast alike. They both certainly deserved a day off from all their hard work.

The custom of the day was to give them the same food ration or even a little more as a reward for a good workweek. Then farmers began to notice a physical change in their draft horses by Monday morning. The horses became stiff, and it was obvious they showed symptoms of muscle pain. The scientific name for this phenomenon is called *Equine extertional rhabdomyolisis*, or Monday morning disease. Veterinarians and animal nutritionists determined the cause was from the practice of overfeeding the horses on their day off. During the week, horses burned off the energy they consumed from their feed. But on their day off, too many carbohydrates negatively affected their muscles. They physically stiffened up and began to shut down due to the pain associated with the overload of sugars. The remedy was to cut back their rations on days they were not working. It's all about intake and exertion balance.

Scriptural References

The term "horse," "horses," or "horse's" shows up 150 times in the Bible. Most of the time it is in reference to military strength or related to battles. *Isaiah 31:1* tells us that some misplaced their trust in God: *"Woe to them that go down to Egypt for help; and stay on horses, and trust in chariots, because they are many; and in horsemen, because they are very strong; but they look not unto the Holy One of Israel; neither seek the Lord!"* See appendix 3 for a list of all the scriptural references.

Spiritual Application

Whether a human or a horse, proper nutrition is required for maintaining a healthy body and is essential for growth. Getting too much food than what the body needs leads to an unhealthy nutritional balance. Christians today may just be experiencing Monday morning disease. They get good, sound preaching on Sunday and become stiff and lethargic on Monday, Tuesday, and the rest of the week. They simply aren't exercising the truths they were fed on Sunday.

The writer of Hebrews speaks to this very subject of improper balance in the believers' spiritual diet and exercise routine. They were once eating solid spiritual food, but now can only digest simple, basic spiritual food.

> *For though by this time you ought to be teachers, you need someone to teach you again the basic principles of the oracles of God. You need milk, not solid food. (Hebrews 5:12)*

Let me ask you a few bold questions that are running through my head and heart. As I ask you these questions, I am asking myself as well:

1. Have you shared Christ's saving love with anyone in the past month?
2. How has God specifically answered your prayers in the last month?
3. What has God been teaching you through your personal Bible study in the last month?

If you can answer these questions, giving details and testimony of all He is doing in and through you, then you are spiritually following your diet and exercise plan that fits your spiritual nutrition. Congratulations! Enjoy the "solid food" found in the scriptures that allows you to feast on the meat of the Word. If you answered, "Not in the last month, but it used to be like that some ten or twelve years ago," then your spiritual intake has far exceeded your exercise output and you've become out of shape.

We should be witnessing, studying, and praying every day. Does it seem like God isn't speaking to you anymore? Have you felt He doesn't open doors for witnessing about His saving grace to others? God has been waiting patiently for you to move on to solid food and for your exercise routine to be in line with what He wants for you.

Owl (Bubo virginianus)

Common Name: Great Horned Owl

Background

Sometimes known as a hoot owl, this is by far the most common and largest owl of North America. Great horned owls are uniquely adaptable birds of prey. They can live beyond twenty years and most of the time will select mates for life. They do not necessarily raise young every year.

Owls swallow their smaller prey whole. The larger animals will be picked apart and consumed or fed to the young owlets. They regurgitate pellets made up of bones, fur, and undigested body parts. The pellets are cast out near their hunting perch. During my college wildlife class, we dissected these pellets to determine what the owl consumed. Most of their diet consists of mice or moles, but they have also found pellets showing amphibians, fish, reptiles, and squirrels. Owls are nocturnal, hunting and feeding after dark.

Their concave, saucer-shaped face functions much like a satellite dish, helping them to focus on sounds. Although not true, owls appear to be able to turn their head completely around. They can only turn them 270 degrees. This aids in listening for prey to enhance their ability to discern where they are. As the owl sits patiently on a limb or perch, it scans the ground for sounds and focuses on noises. They are always watching and listening. Their ear tufts are merely decorative. They have ears, but they are located on the sides of their head.

Scriptural References

The Bible lists the word "owl" or "owls" sixteen times, and each are found only in the Old Testament. See appendix 3 for the scriptural references.

Spiritual Application

One of the great promises found in the Bible is repeated several times: "*I will never leave you, nor forsake you*" (*Hebrews 13:5*). Another is *2 Chronicles 16:9*: "*For the eyes of the LORD run to and fro throughout the whole earth, to give strong support to those whose heart is blameless towards Him.*" Once we acknowledge Him as the one true God and accept His work of salvation for us on the cross of Calvary, we read that He is always watching. This is not done in a vengeful way, but as a caring parent would with their children. God is always watching, always there! What a comforting thought it is to know that God encompasses us.

The owl, sitting on its perch, is created to focus its eyes and ears on what is happening on the ground. At an infinitely higher degree, God is on His throne focusing on what is happening on the earth. He isn't some god who sits back and observes us from a distance. He came and dwelt among us because He wants to have fellowship with us, His creation.

Let's explore this thought of God encompassing us from scripture:

- "*The LORD Himself goes before you*" (*Deuteronomy 31:8*). God heads down your life's path, blazing a trail to show you the way you should go.
- "*Know therefore today, and lay it to your heart, that the LORD is God in heaven above and on the earth beneath, there is no other*" (*Deuteronomy 4:39*). God is in heaven above us watching, and He is below with us, encouraging us.

- *"For I, the LORD your God, hold your right hand; it is I who says to you, 'Fear not, I am the one who helps you'"* (*Isaiah 41:13*). If the Creator of everything is holding my hand, then He is beside me.
- *"Men of stature shall come over to you and be yours. They will plead with you saying, 'Surely, God is in you'"* (*Isaiah 45:14*). When a Christian is following God and living righteously, people will see something different about how they conduct their life and see Christ living in you. Live a life that draws others to Christ.
- *"As I was on my way and drew near to Damascus, about noon a great light from heaven shown around me"* (*Acts 26:13*). God's very presence encompassed Saul as he was about to be transformed into the man God wanted him to be.

The owl is created with special abilities to see and hear to capture food for itself, its mate, and its young. God, on the other hand, sees and hears to have fellowship with us. He goes before us. He is above and below us. He is at our side, holding our hand. He is in us. He shines His light all around us. Oh, how He must love us!

Oxen (Bos primigenius)

Common Name: Ox

Background

The ox has been a beast of burden for thousands of years. Once Adam was expelled from the Garden of Eden, he had to work the land by the sweat of his brow. I am sure it didn't take long after the fall to harness the power of animals to help him tend the fields and pull heavy loads.

A team of oxen cannot be randomly hitched together to perform a task such as pulling a wagon. The training begins only weeks after being born. Calves are selected similar in size and even color. Many times, twins are used and yoked together. Everything must be done together. Eating, drinking, walking, standing, and laying down are all coordinated as one. They no longer exist as individuals. The yoke binds them together and trains them to think and respond as one. If they remained individuals in their actions, nothing would get accomplished.

It is extremely hard to train two different species to work together as a draft team. Both a donkey and an ox can be trained to pull a cart, but not together. Mentally, they must be trained using different methods and signals. Their physical pairing doesn't complement each other. This will cause skin to develop sores and muscles to become fatigued.

Deuteronomy 22:10 gives this warning, "*You shall not yoke an ox and a donkey.*" Trying to force together such an unlikely pair will only accomplish frustration between the animals and the trainer. It just doesn't work.

I have walked behind a team of oxen plowing the ground. It isn't easy, and thankfully, the team was better at it than I was. Whoever was responsible for their training deserved a lot of credit. It takes years of dedication and patience to make the two individual animals think and react exactly as the driver expects them to act.

Scriptural Reference

"Ox" or "oxen" appears 153 times in the Bible, making it the fourth most common animal mentioned. It is referred to in two ways: a beast of burden that can often represent wealth or it refers to one of the designated "clean" animals allowed to be eaten under the Jewish law. See appendix 3 for a complete list of references.

Spiritual Application

There are several good applications we can get from learning about the ox.

First and foremost, it is important to realize that God alone should be our trainer and driver. The team or the single ox cannot adequately discipline itself. Once we get this principle down, our training is easier.

Second, let's consider this notion of trying to pair up an unsuitable team. The Old Testament verse in *Deuteronomy 22:10* has a New Testament companion text that takes it right to the spiritual level. *2 Corinthians 6:14* tells us not to be unequally yoked. This concept isn't dealing just with animal husbandry from an agricultural use. It is dealing with a deeper principle, namely our relationships. A donkey is considered unclean under Jewish law and unfit for humans to eat. The ox is clean and acceptable to eat. The clean and the unclean should not be yoked together.

In the Corinthian passage, the believer (clean) shall not be yoked together with the unbeliever (unclean). One of the things Paul was trying to tell the carnal Christians in Corinthians was that their fellowships, business partners, and marriages were spiritually diabolic toward each other. Starting with marriage and working your way down the "things that matter most" list, believers shall not be yoked or bound with unbelievers.

Third, like a well-trained team of oxen, believers hear and respond to the Master or Driver. They know the commands and signals and follow them. The unbeliever doesn't respond to the commands or reacts in opposition to them. Being unequally yoked in marriage, business partners, and close friendships is a constant pull against each other. This results in efforts that only chaff the skin and fatigues the muscles. Nothing much can get accomplished.

Prior to dating and marriage, we should have the mind-set that unbelievers aren't an option. They aren't what God says is best for us. For those that already find themselves in an unequally yoked situation, realize that it will be a struggle and you will have to be strong to pull in a godly direction. It will be hard, but the unbelieving one might eventually yield their spirit over to Christ.

Our pastor often quotes a phrase from an unknown source:

> There's only two choices on the shelf;
> Pleasing God, or pleasing self.

You can avoid an awful lot of pain and struggles by taking advice from scripture. Be equally yoked as a matching set of oxen in order that two are working together as one to please Him!

Peacock (Pavo cristatus)

Common Name: Peacock

Background

The male peacock has one of the most flamboyant displays of plumage of all the birds. After he attracts the attention of a peahen, he entices her with his ornate spreading presentation of his tail feathers. He vibrates his breast feathers, which makes a sort of electric humming sound. The tail feathers can be as much as five feet long. They have a variety of colors and patterns that have made peacock feathers a sought-after commodity for years.

Only the male is called a peacock. The females are called peahens and are part of the pheasant family of birds. They collectively are called peafowl. They are native to Asia and are threatened due to habitat loss, predation, and smuggling. Peafowl are omnivores, meaning they eat both plants and small animals such as insects, arthropods, and amphibians. They have a lifespan of twenty years.

There is another side of the peacock that almost negates its ornate beauty. They have a very loud and obnoxious cry. Seeing them at a zoo or animal park is one thing. Living near a party of peafowl can cause a nuisance issue. Despite having a long train of tail feathers, they can easily take flight and will land in treetops or rooftops to avoid capture.

Asians traditionally associated peacock feathers with immortality. They believed that owning peacock feathers provided a doorway to spiritual guidance. It was once believed that the flesh of a dead peacock would not decay. Hence, the early Christian church used

95

them as decorations during Easter as a symbol that Christ did not remain dead.

Scriptural References

"Peacock" is found only three times in the scriptures. You can read the accounts in *1 Kings 10:22*, *2 Chronicles 9:21*, and *Job 39:13*. The first two references seem to imply an imported creature. The verse in Job could possibly be describing an ostrich.

Spiritual Application

Many people understand the phrase "dressed to impress." I think the peacock must have gotten the memo a long time ago. But like the peacock, people dress up for special occasions such as weddings, proms, and other formal events. There is absolutely nothing wrong with looking your best and having nice clothes. But who you are isn't defined by how you dress or how you look. Remember, God knows the heart (*Psalm 139:23*).

> *Showing all good faith that they may adorn the doctrine of God our Savior in every respect. (Titus 2:10)*

The word "adorn" in Greek is *kosmeo*, and it means "to put in order" or "to decorate." It is where we get our English word "cosmetics."

The Christian should be doctrinally "dressed for success." As believers we need to adorn ourselves with the teachings of God. As a woman would put on cosmetics to make herself more presentable in public, we should be living our outward lives in a way that is not in conflict with biblical truths. We are given all the cosmetics needed for a complete spiritual makeover when we accepted Christ as our Savior. The teachings found within the pages of the Bible are given to us to put in order or "put on." For godly doctrinal beauty to be seen openly by the world, they must be applied internally. We take them in, they change us inwardly, and they change our outward appearance.

Here is a list of the things we need to "put on" so that we decorate ourselves in the doctrine of God:

- *"But put on the Lord Jesus Christ"* (*Romans 13:14*).
- *"For as many as you as were baptized into Christ have put on Christ"* (*Galatians 3:27*).
- *"And who has also put His seal on us and given us His Spirit in our hearts as a guarantee"* (*2 Corinthians 1:22*).
- *"Put on the whole armor of God, that you may be able to stand against the schemes of the devil"* (*Ephesians 6:11*).
- *"And to put on the new self, created after the likeness of God in true righteousness and holiness"* (*Ephesians 4:24*).
- *"Put on then, as God's chosen ones, holy and beloved, compassionate hearts, kindness, humility, meekness and patience"* (*Colossians 3:12*).
- *"And above all these put on love, which binds everything together in perfect harmony"* (*Colossians 3:14*).

Seeing a peacock in full display of his ornate feathers pales in comparison to seeing a child of God fully adorning the doctrines of God in every respect. By doing this, the whole world sees our eternal beauty because we choose to put on Christ.

Pigeon (Columbia livia)

Common Name: Pigeon

Background

Rarely found alone, pigeons tend to flock together. They can be considered a nuisance bird living in cities and rural areas alike. Some people keep pigeons and engage them in competitive races, clocking their flights back to their coop.

They have a keen, sharp eyesight that is far better than man's. Pigeons have been used in search and rescue missions over open waters. Before heat-sensory equipment existed, planes were once fitted with bubble domes underneath with a pigeon enclosed in the sphere to provide an unobstructed view of the water. Their reaction to movement can be electronically monitored to identify when they spot movement such as a survivor waving their hands for help. Their eyesight can single out an object in a sea of moving waves.

Thirty some years ago, I was doing an apprenticeship with a master falconer. He was preparing to livetrap and tag red-tailed hawks during their fall migration. He had permission to capture, band, and keep two of them, but he needed bait for the trap site located in the mountains of southern Pennsylvania. I knew where I could catch feral pigeons from a few farms. They were not only used for bait for a hungry hawk; but also for their keen eyesight.

As we sat in a camouflaged blind, one by one the pigeons were placed in the trap to lure in first passage birds of prey. Our vision was already poor, but was more restricted in the confines of a blind. The only view we had was the trap where the pigeon was tethered. Watching the pigeon prepared us for action. As the pigeon caught sight of an incoming bird far off in the northern horizon, we could see it hunker down and try to hide. The day proved to be successful as we left with two juvenile birds to be trained for hunting. I expected it to be a good day when the first bird we lured in was an impressive golden eagle.

The pigeon, like many other birds, has binocular vision that permits them to use focal spots behind their eyes to increase their ability to see further and with more clarity. They can "zoom in" on an object such as a person waving in the ocean or a predator far off in the distance.

Scriptural References

"Pigeons" are found eleven times in scripture and exclusively in the Old Testament. They are recognized in the Jewish religious ritual of offering sacrifices. See appendix 3 for a complete list of references.

Spiritual Application

Our human eyes are quite limited as compared to that of birds like the pigeon. However, born-again believers have been given keener eyesight for things that matter to God. Having the Holy Spirit dwelling inside us improves our spiritual vision. Let's face it, our previous eyesight was nowhere near twenty-twenty. We see better now and can focus on the important things of this world. *Matthew 13:16* tells it like it is: "*But Blessed are your eyes, for they see, and your ears, for they hear.*" Like the pigeons used to rescue lives at sea, I pray that we use our God-given keener eyesight to help see those that need to be spiritually rescued. I also pray that we zoom in on the right focal points rather than being distracted by things that don't matter.

The old Irish hymn tells it best in the song "Be Thou My Vision":

> *Be Thou my vision oh Lord of my heart,*
> *Nought be all else to me, save that Thou art;*
> *Thou best thought by day or by night,*
> *Waking or sleeping, Thy presence my light.*

Quail (Colinus virginianus)

Common Name: Northern Bobwhite

Background

Quail are a small game bird that used to populate in the northeast United States. Their common name, bobwhite, hints to the sound of the call it makes. In the wild, quail have many enemies. They are low on the food chain and more than humans find them tasty. In the early 1970s a late spring frost destroyed the unhatched eggs in many of the clutches. Since that decline, farming practices and urban sprawl have consumed much of the quail's natural habitat. The good news is that wildlife conservation organizations have been actively working with farmers, landowners, and sportsman groups to establish new coveys every year.

One winter morning after a significant snowfall, the landscape out my living room window was covered with a fresh blanket of snow. The only place that didn't have snow was under our picnic table. I watched as the normal visitors flocked to our bird feeder. Then I noticed five larger birds making their way along the ground to pick through the seed cast out by the picky blue jays. These were quail. I had never seen quail come to our bird feeder before. They were very eager to get an easy meal.

After having their fill of the discarded seed, they gathered underneath the picnic table to rest on the bare ground. The table-top provided excellent cover from any predators coming from above. Only the sides were exposed. One by one each quail became settled in a formation that provided maximum protection for the small covey. They all faced outward in a tight circle, with their tail feathers pointing inward. They formed a ring of protection for warmth and defense.

An individual quail was not able to watch all the exposed sides while the others rested. So each took a percentage of the circle and kept vigil over their own sector. They rested there about an hour and quietly moved on top of the newly fallen snow. They had protected each other by being diligent to watch what was right in front of them.

Scriptural Reference

"Quail" are only used four times in scripture: *Exodus 16:13*, *Numbers 11:31* and *32*, and *Psalm 105:40*. You probably already know the main context of quail found in the Bible. They were used as food for the Israelite nation while they wandered in the desert. They were given by Jehovah Jira, God our Provider.

Spiritual Application

As I sat and watched the quail that snowy winter's day, it made me think of the rebuilding of the walls around Jerusalem by the prompting of Nehemiah. The city walls laid in ruins, and their enemies were taunting them, saying that even if you rebuild the walls, they would be so weak that they would crumble to the ground if a fox ran across them. The Gentile nations were opposed to the thought of Israel regaining the stronghold she once had. They remembered how the God of Israel protected them and fought for them to take possession of the land. Sandballot did not want them to succeed and repeatedly tried to stop them.

Nehemiah came up with a brilliant strategy. He assigned certain people to work on the gates and others to work on the portion of the wall near their ancestral homes. God let Nehemiah know that the people would work hardest near their family property to make sure the wall was solidly built. They did excellent workmanship to repair what was right in front of them.

The second thing Nehemiah did can be found in *Nehemiah 4:15–17*, where it says, "*When our enemies heard that it was known to us and that God had frustrated their plan, we all returned to the wall, each one to their own work. From that day on, half of my servants worked on construction and half held the spears, shields, bows and coat of mail. And the leaders stood behind the whole house of Judah, who were building the wall. Those who carried burdens were loaded in such a way that each labored on the work with one hand and held his weapon with the other.*"

Here we see laborers pulling double duty working on the wall and protecting their property and each other. Imagine being part of a short-term mission trip organized to construct a building project in a hostile country with much opposition. The amazing part as stated in *Nehemiah 6:15* was that the project was completed in fifty-two days. As an individual, Nehemiah couldn't do the work. But as a team, the work was completed faster than expected.

Like the quail in my yard on that winter's day, we need to focus on our own responsibilities and do our fair share of the work. We need to empower others to do the same and trust that they will do it. There is plenty of work to be done for the cause of Christ. We can be an encouragement to others by doing our work and collectively carry out the task to completion. Being busy without a purpose has no purpose. Let's stay focused on the task that lie right before us. Let's witness to the ones God has sent our way. Let's befriend the helpless and hopeless. Let's take the gospel message to those right in front of us and not leave it to others. If we all do our reasonable service, the kingdom will be built, the workers will be encouraged, and God will be glorified.

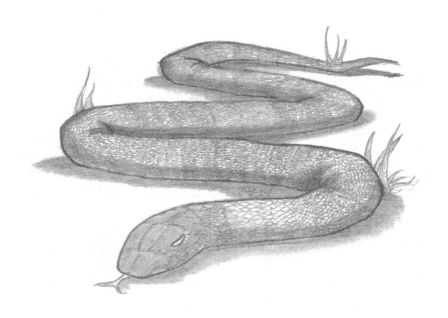

Serpent (Elaphe obsoleta)

Common Name: Black Snake, Black Rat Snake

Background

Call me crazy, but I find it hard to resist picking up a black snake when I see one on my property. Usually, I release it near my barn. Sure, any snake startles me at first because there are copperheads and timber rattlers where I live. But once I correctly identify what kind of snake it is, I calm down. Black snakes are welcome in my barn to help keep the mouse population under control. I routinely find shed skins every year. My children are used to seeing me with a black snake coiled around my arm. I have been told that most people aren't as receptive to snake as I am. Yep! Call me crazy!

Another good reason for keeping black snakes around is that they keep other snakes such as copperheads away. It may be an old wives' tale, but since releasing black snakes in my barn, I haven't seen any copperheads. I've identified eight different species of snakes on my property over twenty-nine years.

Black snakes can grow to be eight feet long. They can climb up stone walls and trees. They feed mostly on mice, moles, shrews, and voles, but they also like eggs and other small animals. The female can lay one to two dozen eggs per year that usually hatch in August. The number of eggs directly relates to the age of the snake.

There are four ways to determine if a snake is poisonous or not:

1. Nonpoisonous snake's scales will have more of a shine to them, and they will not show a divisional line on the underside or belly.
2. Poisonous snakes have pits on the sides of their head, whereas nonpoisonous snakes do not.
3. Nonpoisonous snakes have round pupils or eyes. Poisonous snakes have elliptical pupils.
4. The shape of a poisonous snake's head is more triangular and reduces at the beginning of the body of the snake. In nonpoisonous species, there is very little shape difference between head and body. In all three cases, you need to be up close and examine the snakes.

I've been told by many people that they don't share my level of tolerance for snakes of any kind. A common expression around here is, "The only good snake is…" Well, you know how the rest of that goes. The fact is, most people have a downright hatred of snakes. However, we should see how they fill an important part of our created ecosystem.

Scriptural Reference

There are several animals that fall under the heading of "serpent" or "snake." The combination of all these make up seventy-one references. They include the following:

- "Adder(s)" found five times.
- "Asp(s)" found five times.
- "Serpent(s)" found fifty-three times.
- "Viper(s)" found eight times.

Some of the references to "serpent" are indirect names to Satan or the devil, which obviously was not part of the created animals. He was part of the angelic host and aspired to be like the Most

High and was cast out of heaven. See the complete list of references found in appendix 3.

Spiritual Application

From the fall of mankind in the Garden of Eden and the curse placed upon the serpent to have to crawl on their belly for the rest of their existence, snakes have been linked with evil. The term "cunning" found throughout scriptures is an adjective that focuses on the craftsmanship of fine work. But when applied to the serpent, it is more like the skill of craftiness or deceitfulness. The account of the serpent in the Garden of Eden depicts the later use of the word.

> *Now the serpent was more crafty than any other beast of the field that the Lord God had made. (Genesis 3:1)*

Later on in that same chapter we read:

> *The Lord God said to the serpent, "Because you have done this, cursed are you above all livestock and above all beast of the field; on your belly you shall go, and dust you shall eat all the days of your life. I will put enmity between you and the woman, and between your offspring and her offspring; He shall bruise your head and you shall bruise His heel." (Genesis 3:14–15)*

God cursed the serpent who would have originally walked upright and put "enmity" between humans and snakes. So what is enmity? Some might think it means "fear," but that isn't quite correct. The Hebrew word here means "hostility" or "hatred." This hostility or hatred is extended to all humans and all snakes. It isn't expressed as a good and godly relationship to have. It is part of the curse. So is hatred a bad emotion? Are we inoculated with hatred because of the curse? The answer to both those questions is no.

Hatred is one of our created emotions. We find several places in scripture where God hates things. *Proverbs 6:16–19* gives us a list of seven things God hates:

1. A proud look.
2. A lying tongue.
3. Hands that shed innocent blood.
4. A heart that devises wicked plans.
5. Feet that run quickly toward evil.
6. A false witness that speaks lies.
7. A person that sows discord among the brethren.

Basically, we can sum up what this passage in Proverbs is saying into one concise statement: God hates sin! These things are reminiscent of the last six things written in *Exodus 20*, otherwise known as the Ten Commandments. So there are things we can have hatred for, but we must guard ourselves against letting our hatred become misplaced.

What does this have to do with whether I like or hate snakes? It is a result of the fall and the preceding curse that brings this undesirable emotion against snakes. Some people are consumed with so much fear and hatred toward snakes that they can't even function normally. They lose all self-control. That all comes as part of the curse. How should we react to things we are fearful of or show hatred toward?

What is the prescribed remedy against this emotional feeling that is part of the curse?

2 Timothy 1:7 says, "*For God has given us a spirit not of fear but of power and love and self-control.*"

Hate the things that God has hated, not the things He has created!

Sheep (Ovis aries)

Common Name: Sheep

Background

Sheep were one of the first animals to become domesticated. They have been raised by man for thousands of years and are nearly dependent on man for their survival. It is hard to put an exact number of different breeds, but it is over five hundred worldwide. Sheep have been selectively bred for their different traits. Some are raised for their wool and even further selected for wool carpet versus wool clothing. There are breeds of sheep raised to produce milk for Rutherford cheese. Still others are raised for quality meat production. Sheep have been a viable part of agricultural commerce for man for as long as mankind has been around.

Livestock production classes were very much part of my college degree. One of the many classes was meat processing, where students learned how to make the different cuts of meat. During this course, students learned how to distinguish lamb from mutton.

Lamb is meat from a young animal that provides a tender quality. Mutton, on the other hand, is from older sheep, and the meat can be tough. Dr. Ziegler explained to us how that the break joint is a cartilaginous part of the shank just above the ankle in lambs that ossifies as the animal matures. If the sheep is young, the break joint has not fused together to become a solid bone. The presence of the break joint in the leg of lamb would define the age of the carcass. An informed buyer would know if they are getting lamb or mutton. The price is considerably higher for lamb, but sellers would try to sneak in mutton for the higher price if they could.

Another interesting fact about the break joint is as a management tool in raising lambs. In every group of lambs, you would have one or two that would be headstrong and wander off on their own. When this happens, the shepherd would intentionally "break" this joint, causing the ligaments to hyperextend. This renders the lamb immobile, and the shepherd would have to carry the lamb everywhere for weeks. By the time the leg heals, the lamb would have bonded with the shepherd and would never wander away from the flock.

Scriptural Reference

In one form or another, "sheep" have nearly eight hundred references in the Bible. There are five different terms used:

- "Ewe" found 10 times.
- "Lamb(s)" found 166 times.
- "Ram(s)" found 145 times.
- "Sheep" found 286 times.
- "Flock(s)" found 187 times.

The term "flocks" usually applies to sheep. See the complete list of references found in appendix 3.

Spiritual Application

With so many scriptural references about sheep, there are plenty of things that can be expounded upon for personal application. For instance, when John the Baptist saw Jesus coming toward him, he proclaimed, *"Behold the Lamb of God who takes away the sins of the world"* (*John 1:29*). He was the spotless Lamb whose blood was shed, once and for all of mankind.

But let's take a closer look and consider this thought of using the break joint in the lambs to create a deeper bond between the shepherd and his sheep. In Luke 15:4 we see the familiar passage where Jesus explains of the shepherd that leaves the ninety-nine to go rescue the one that wandered off. This act of urgency and love shows the compassion Jesus has for each of us.

> *But God shows His love for us that while we were*
> *still sinners, Christ died for us. (Romans 5:8)*

When we were determined to stray from the protection of the flock and the Shepherd, God pursued us, rescued us, and died for us.

Christmastime is festive, and I like seeing all the decorations in people's homes, churches, and stores. One of my favorite is seeing the nativity scene. If you have one of these in your home or church, it probably includes figurines. Chances are, it includes a shepherd with a lamb draped over his shoulders and being carried. That figurine depicts the break joint being used. It recounts that the wayward lamb has been found, temporarily debilitated, but is in the healing process to build a closer bond with the shepherd.

Jesus, our Good Shepherd, takes us at our most disobedient time and shows us His love for us. He cares for us. He carries us. He leads us to the best places that provide care and protection. In the example of the shepherd using the break joint in the lamb, it is important to notice that the shepherd cannot use this method of discipline with older sheep. The shank bone is fused, and it will cause major damage to the sheep. The longer we spend wandering off on our own and the older we become, the harder it is to trust in and rely upon our Shepherd, Jesus Christ. The older we get, the harder our hearts become and the more likely we will reject God. That is why we should seek the Lord while we are still young.

"Come, Thy Fount" was written by Robert Robinson, who must have been inspired by understanding that we are all like sheep. Here are a few lines from his familiar hymn:

> *Jesus sought me when a stranger, wandering from the fold of God;*
> *He to rescue me from danger, Interposed His precious blood.*
> *Prone to wander—Lord, I feel it—Prone to leave the God I love;*
> *Here's my heart—O take and seal it, Seal it for thy courts above.*

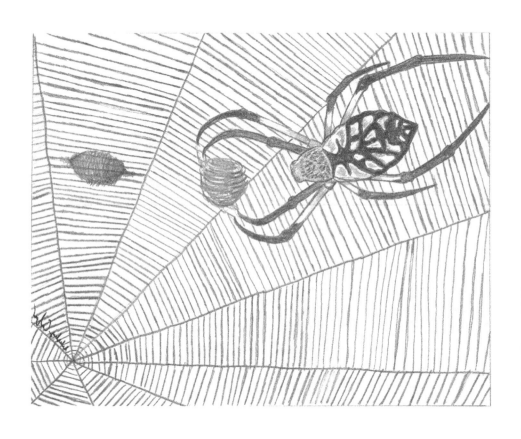

116

Spider (Argiope aurantia)

Common Name: Garden Spider

Background

Ever since I was a young kid, I loved to take hikes. When I grew up, I got paid to walk around on people's properties to look at their land to offer conservation alternatives on their land. On one such farm, I remember walking with the owner as we traded groans of disgust when we each took multiple turns walking face-first right into spiderwebs. Why does it always seem that no matter your height, the spider's web is always face high? You claw and rub your head hoping to get the spider, dead insects, and all the web off your face and out of your hair. That day, we each must have had spider facials at least five times. We complained and tried to avoid them as much as possible, but did we ever stop to think how much effort it took that spider to construct her web? There are some amazing facts regarding a spider's web that we need to learn to appreciate, especially if we are going to just walk right into them.

Spiderwebs are magnificent engineered structures. The uniformity of the gaps between the silks are nearly perfect. A spider spins several different types of silks to make up the web structure. She starts off with the thicker anchor silks that provide the basic support. Other silks are spun with a sticky coating to make the flying insects adhere to the web. Still another type of silk is used to wrap up the prey to preserve it for a food source later.

Spiders use different glands in their body to make these different threads of silk. At the lower end of their abdomen, spiders have several glands that excrete the different silk types. It's the same spider, but different silks.

Scriptural References

The KJV of the Bible has three references to spiders. They are *Job 8:14*, *Proverbs 30:28*, and *Isaiah 59:5*. In Job and Isaiah it looks at the spider's web. The Proverbs reference in some translations uses lizard instead of spider. Either case, it doesn't change the imagery of the message.

Spiritual Application

God, in His great wisdom, has equipped each believer with spiritual gifts. No one gift is more important than any of the others. It is possible that a person might possess more than one gift. These gifts are given so that the body of believers can use them in the local church to fulfill the work God has called for them. Just as in the spider, all silks are needed to build a sound structure. Without the support or anchor threads, the entire web would fail. Equally important are the silks used to hold and wrap the insects.

God has given these different gifts for the edification of the church. We find in *1 Corinthians 12:4–7*, "N*ow there are a variety of gifts, but the same spirit, and there are varieties of service, but the same Lord, and there are a variety of activities, but the same God who empowers them all in everyone. To each is given the manifestation of the spirit for the common good.*"

It is the same Spirit, the same Lord, and the same God; but a variety of gifts are given. We must use the gifts God has given us to support His work in our local churches or in the mission field He has called us into. The spider's web is only effective when all the silks are properly used. It is the same with our spiritual gifts and the church. Go and spin your silks as an example to others.

> *But set the believers an example in speech, in conduct, in love, in faith, in purity. (1 Timothy 4:12)*

The basic information about the spider's different silks came from a monthly magazine called *Answers* magazine. "The purpose of *Answers* magazine is to illustrate the importance of Genesis in building a creation-based worldview, and to equip readers with practical answers so they can confidently communicate the gospel and biblical authority with accuracy and graciousness." Their work can be found at www.AnswersinGenesis.org.

Stork (Mycteria americana)

Common Name: Wood Stork

Background

These large wading birds are probably most familiar as the deliverer of babies in folklore. The birds live in colonies called rookeries in tree canopies. Swamps and marshes are their homes. Very little historically was known about storks until 1957 when all known nesting sites produced no young that year. This occurred because of a severe drought that dried up most of the waterways. The lack of water depleted their main source of food, freshwater fish.

Habitat destruction is the biggest threat to storks today. Drained swamps and increased demand for lumber have competed for the bird's nesting and feeding sites. Because of their communal style of living, they are competing against themselves for habitat.

The adults pair off during mating and construct large nests in the tree canopy. Each nest can produce three to four eggs. After the eggs are properly incubated and hatched, the parents are kept busy supplying the young with fresh fish. Storks will catch as much as fifty pounds of fresh fish for every one of their offspring.

The young birds are effective at warding off predators. They use their long, sharp bills to pinch and peck their aggressors. When this fails, they will spit up their entire stomach contents. It is not certain if this is a natural defense reaction or done out of nervousness. Either way, it is effective in keeping predators away, and we can see why human interaction is rare.

The rookeries are a safe haven for the stork. Parents share the responsibility of collectively raising their young. On the ground, storks look and appear awkward. Yet in the air, their natural beauty is matched by their impressive size. Their wide wing span is equaled by the length of their trailing feet and the S-shaped neck.

Scriptural Reference

The stork is mentioned five times and only in the Old Testament: *Leviticus 11:19, Deuteronomy 14:18, Psalm 104:17, Jeremiah 8:7,* and *Zechariah 5:9.*

Spiritual Application

Insects are known to live in colonies, but very few animals live this way. The stork collectively co-exist, even to their own detriment. What examples can we find in scripture that express this idea? Nimrod was known as the hunter. His prey was not wild game. He was a hunter of people. He wanted all the elite to live in his city. So he gathered up all the intelligentsia of his day to live in a commune. The book of Genesis tells us the extent of the abilities of these ancient people.

Genesis 11:6 says, *"And the Lord said, Behold the people is one, and they have all one language; and this they began to do; and now nothing will be restrained from them, which they have imagined to do."*

Think of it. All that they imagined, they could do. The sky's the limit! So that is what they went after. They decided to use their intellectual gifts to construct a tower up to God. They went right for the top. So what is wrong with having lofty goals and ambitions? They were told by God to disperse and fill the earth. Instead, they disobeyed God to their own detriment. The storks compete among themselves, vying for the same habitat. The carrying capacity can only support a certain number of storks because it will have an effect on the rest of the environment. Freshwater fish numbers will be reduced, and like a chain reaction, the local plant and wildlife community will be unsustainable.

Sociologists have claimed that the entire world's population could exist in a city the size of the state of Texas. That would leave the rest of the world available for growing food and having wildlife sanctuaries. The problem is, everyone living in that large of a footprint would exceed the carrying capacity of that area, and the natural order of things would be out of control. God has given man dominion over the earth. This charge is for man to be stewards of all the resources this world has to offer. We are not to hoard up for ourselves treasures that will rot, rust, and waste away. We are to store up for ourselves treasures in heaven where they are preserved for all of eternity.

Like the stork, humanity looks awkward here on earth. We were created for something much more than simply existing. Our natural beauty will be seen when we are translated into our eternal bodies and in our natural habitat, heaven. And when that day comes, it will be glorious!

Tortoise (Terrapene carolina)

Common Name: Box Turtle

Background

The most common land turtle in the northeast United States is the box turtle. These reptiles have attracted the attention of many of young kids. They are known by their classic domed shell that is hinged at the bottom front. The carapace, or shell, gives it a rather unique defense mechanism. When startled or under attack, it draws itself into its shell and closes the hinge for protection.

Scientist estimate that box turtles can live to be one hundred years old or more. It is said that you can count the number of plate layers to get their age. However, the plates can wear away over time. So numbers over twenty-five are considered best guesses. The box turtle hibernates during the cold northeast winters. They dig a hole and stay tucked away underground until the temperature of the soil warms enough for them to come out.

There are two ways to tell the difference between males and females. One way is to look at the color of their eyes. Males tend to have orange or red eyes, and females have brown. The other way to tell is to look at the under-portion of their shell. If there is a predominant indentation in the middle of the shell, it is most likely a male.

Box turtles are most comfortable in forests and meadows. Their most common enemy is a highway. Even though they do have some natural predators, death by being run over is among the highest reason for loss of life. By the time they slowly make their way onto a road, they are at risk. As many as 30 percent lose their life due to traffic fatalities.

We all know turtles move slowly, but there is something they cannot do. They cannot look back. Turtles expel a lot of energy and time trying to turn around. So they learn to accept what is behind them and move forward. Turtles tend to focus on what lies before them.

Scriptural Reference

"Tortoise" is found only once in the KJV Bible, *Leviticus 11:29*. From Hebrew, it would likely compare more to a land turtle or lizard rather than a sea turtle. These creatures are all considered unclean and not allowed for human consumption under the Levitical law.

Spiritual Application

There are many figures in history to admire. Some of them we wish we could be like more than others. Too many times, the figures we elevate high on a pedestal often slip up and let us down. The Bible has examples of ordinary men that allowed sin to creep into their lives and drag the name of God down. Jonah, Samson, Moses, and David come to mind. There are many more to be listed, and we might as well go ahead and put our names right down there with them. But there are a few good examples that God shows us. Still, we need to understand that as good as they seemed to be, they were sinners who needed salvation.

If there is one example that sticks out in my mind, it would be Elisha. When I read of the special way he was called by God into the ministry of being a prophet, I find it hard to see anything other than a complete and obedient servant. Reading of the events of his calling in *1 Kings 19:19–21*, we are shown a man of obvious wealth. To possess twelve teams of oxen, the servants needed to drive them, and the fields large enough to utilize all of them for plowing indicates his riches.

Elijah is given guidance to seek out Elisha as his replacement. God shows him where he is as he works alongside his servants. We need to stop right here and point out that Elisha was in the field, laboring right alongside of the hired men. He was a man of humility and of a sound work ethic. I have driven a team of horses before. I admire a person who isn't afraid of hard work. God was preparing Elisha in that field for a time yet to come when he would be breaking up the fallow ground in men's hearts to receive the seed of faith that would yield fruit in due season.

Elijah laid his mantle on Elisha, signifying God's calling on his life. And immediately Elisha answered the call. Like the tortoise, he didn't look back. God had been preparing him to replace Elijah as prophet. Elisha broke up his plow and harness and used them for fuel to make a fire to sacrifice his team of oxen as a symbolic statement for everyone to see that his old life was done. He was leaving his farm, his wealth, and his servants to become a servant of God.

When it came time for Elijah to be taken up to heaven by God, he gave his blessing on Elisha. Elisha instead asked for a double blessing and received it. He went on to do many more miracles than Elijah had done. We are told in 2 *Kings 13:20–21* that after he had died and was buried, a dead man was cast into the grave of Elisha. When the body encountered Elisha's bones, the dead man revived and stood up to his feet.

Once we make that choice to follow God, we should never look back. Choosing to fully embrace the life God has intended for us is our highest calling. Let's learn from this one thing a turtle cannot do and quit looking back. Don't let the past haunt us or halt us from moving forward. If we are blessed to live as long as a turtle, we will have surely made some bad choices along the way. We have a race to finish. We have a prize to obtain. Each forward step brings us closer to Him who has called us.

Unicorn
(Elasmotherium sibiricum)

Common Name: Great One-Horned Unicorn

Background

Of all the creatures contained in the Bible, the unicorn must be the one with the most mystery surrounding it. When word got out that I was writing a book on the animals found in the Bible, the most common question I got was, "How are you going to deal with the unicorns?" My answer was always the same, "Well, you will have to purchase a copy of the book and read it for yourself."

There have been all sorts of explanations and guesses regarding the details of this creature and why it shows up nine times in the King James Version of the Bible. Some say it is just a goat. Others say it is the side view of a cow that you can only view one of the horns. Still others contest that it never really existed in the first place. The truth is, something called a unicorn did exist. How do I know? Because it is found in scripture. So how do we begin to accept the notion that unicorns were real? First off, we need to unpack our preconceived ideas of a white horse with a single spiral horn coming out of its forehead.

Let's think for a moment that unicorns are found only in fairy tales and kid's artwork hanging on the refrigerator. If you throw in a castle, a rainbow, and some glitter, you have the makings of a really nice fantasy. However, you need to approach the scriptures carefully without picking and choosing what is or isn't real.

If the biblical accounts of unicorns were all wrong, then how do we know which passages are right? Granted, the Bible contains metaphors, poetry, and other literary forms of writing to aid us in understanding God. But the scriptural references we see do not give us any indication that the creature is anything but real.

If you maintain that unicorns are just make-believe, who's to say that the serpent that deceived Adam and Eve was real? If we get to decide what is true in God's Word, we are guilty of thinking ourselves equal to God. If we hijack the authority of God's Word on this or any other subject, we become the deciders of truth. That position will certainly lead us to ruin.

There has been some reasonable chatter lately that the unicorn found in the King James Version could have been a rhinoceros, having a single horn. In fact, if you look up the word "unicorn" in the first Noah Webster dictionary printed in 1828, you will find the word "rhinoceros" in the definition. Likewise, if you look up "rhinoceros," you will find the word "unicorn." Oddly enough, if you look it up in the most recent version of Noah Webster's dictionary, it states "a mystical, horse-like creature with a single horn coming out of its forehead." Words and their meanings have changed over the last two hundred years.

Scriptural References

The word "unicorn" is found nine times in the King James Version of the Bible. In the original 1611 version, a footnote is shown that says, "Or Rhinoceros" (*Numbers 23:22; 24:8; Deuteronomy 33:17; Job 39:9 and 10; Psalm 22:21; 29:6; 92:10; Isaiah 34:7*).

Spiritual Application

If you are someone having difficulty figuring out what is really the unicorn found in the Bible, you are not alone. We as finite beings want to possess knowledge. We spend some thirteen to twenty years or more trying to figure things out. But the important thing to remember is, God is not finite. He is Omniscient (all knowing). In fact, His word breaks it down to a simple, yet complex truth:

> *For as the heavens are higher than the earth, so are*
> *My ways higher than your ways and My thoughts*
> *than your thoughts. (Isaiah 55:9)*

Who says we have to know everything? The fool thinks man is the source of all wisdom. We cannot attempt to hold a candle to the extensive wisdom God possesses.

Romans 1:18–22 says, "*For the wrath of God is revealed from heaven against ungodliness and unrighteousness of men, who by their unrighteousness suppress the truth. For what can be known about God is plain to them, because God has shown it to them. For the invisible attributes, namely His eternal power and divine nature, have been clearly perceived, ever since the creation of the world, in the things that have been made. So they are without excuse. For although they know God, they did not honor Him as God or give thanks to Him, but they became futile in their thinking, and their foolish hearts were darkened. Claiming to be wise, they became fools.*"

Try to humble yourself and accept the fact that some things aren't going to be figured out on this side of heaven. God knows what He created on that sixth day, a unicorn. He created every cell and said it was good. We strain to see through a foggy window for our own selfish desire to know everything. We should be content to wait it out until that day where we shall see Him face-to-face.

We won't be automatically filled with all of God's wisdom. However, isn't it a wonderful thought that throughout all eternity, the mysteries of His creation will be made known to us? I can imagine that "aha" moment when we finally say, "So that's what God's unicorn looks like."

> *For now we see in a mirror dimly, but then face to*
> *face. Now in part, then I shall know fully, even as I*
> *have been fully known. (1 Corinthians 13:12)*

Wolf (Canus lupus)

Common Name: Timber Wolf

Background

The wolf is the largest of the wild dogs. It has been considered incompatible with civilization. It remains the chief predator of domestic livestock, namely sheep and cattle. A single wolf can take down a bison. In the past, they have been hunted, shot, trapped, and poisoned. Normally they are reclusive and stick to the deep woods, away from human contact. But recently, the wolf population is growing and expanding its terrain.

Their habits and diets vary, and they can live off a wide range of food sources to meet their needs. We think of them chasing down large animals such as deer, but they will survive on a steady diet of field mice. They are aggressive hunters and will run in packs, working together to take down the larger animals. Some wolves have become quite famous for their destruction and ability to evade capture. One wolf, called Custer from the South Dakota region, was said to have killed $25,000 worth of sheep and cattle. Another wolf called Three Toes continued to stock his prey for thirteen years and killed over $50,000 worth of livestock.

Wolves generally mate for life, and both adults will care for the young. Females can have anywhere from four to fourteen pups. The average litter is seven. Because they have compatible DNA with domesticated dogs, they have been known to interbreed. Even with this domestic element in their mix, obtaining complete trust in the offspring proves very difficult. They retain their natural instinct and lose their fear of man. These, by far, are the most dangerous.

One of the more vindictive ways to lure a wolf in is to take a very sharp knife and freeze layers of blood on the blade. The knife then is exposed into the open woods by placing it into a snowbank or stump. The blood-thirsty wolf will sniff out the knife and begin licking the blade. The taste of the blood invigorates the wolf to lick with greater intensity. This action will slice the tongue of the wolf, and the fresh blood creates an addictive, self-destructive process. Eventually, the wolf destroys its own body by craving its own lust for blood.

Scriptural Reference

The word "wolf" or "wolves" appears thirteen times in scripture. See appendix 3 for a complete list of reference verses.

Spiritual Application

The wolf is one of the fiercest animals in the Bible. It embodies the thought of sin and lust. A masterful deceiver, lustful desires can stalk a weak Christian until the timing is right to attack and take them down. God's word describes the wolf as a predator to His flocks. Believers are His sheep. In scripture, the wolf symbolizes the enemy or Satan. Often, lust works on us like a well-organized pack of relentless wolves. The lust of the eyes and flesh are difficult to tame. Even the mature Christian isn't exempt from having the effects of lust stalking them at weaker moments. If left to their own desires, these attacks can consume struggling Christians.

God warns us in *Acts 20:29*, "*For I know this, that after my departing shall grievous wolves enter in among you, not sparing the flock.*"

Our churches and Christian homes are not above the attacks of Satan. In fact, some would say that this is where he does some of his best work. Paul knew this danger was facing the Christians of his day, and it remains a threat today. All that lust seeks is a little compromise in our churches or Christian homes. Someone wants things done their own way, and they will stop at nothing to make sure of it. God's way is not considered. They want the church to show tolerance and go along with the world on marriage issues, how the world was created, or when actual life begins. And before long, a strike is made on the church or the Christian family. Some of the sheep are wounded, some are killed, and at the very least, the flock is scattered.

The wise church has a safeguard to keep this from happening. An accountability system is set up where the pastor oversees the congregation, and the congregation prayerfully keeps watch over the pastor. There have been people infiltrating good churches with the intent to spread bad doctrine. They do this rather easily because our churches are always asking for volunteers to teach children's Sunday school classes or vacation Bible school, and we really don't know their full intent. Protection of the flock includes having qualified spiritual leaders in the fold to keep vigil over attacks from within and without. Far too often, churches place trust in the wrong people because they "look" like sheep. Far too often, they are wolves.

The Christian family can safeguard their homes in the same manner as the parent(s) protecting the family and the family holding the parent(s) accountable to their task of raising up godly children.

Matthew 7:15 tells us, *"Beware of false prophets, which come to you in sheep's clothing, but inwardly they are ravening wolves."*

Appendix 1

#	Animals Found in the Bible Animal	King James Version Used References in the Bible
1	Adder	5
2	Ant	1
3	Ass	153
4	Asp	4
5	Badger	14
6	Bats	1
7	Bear	11
8	Beast (general)	334
9	Bees	3
10	Beetle	1
11	Behemoth	1
12	Birds (general)	51
13	Bittern	3
14	Brood	1
15	Bull(s)	12
16	Bullock(s)	137
17	Calf; Calves	48
18	Camel(s)	61
19	Cankerworm	7
20	Caterpillar(s)	9
21	Cattle	149
22	Chameleon	1
23	Chamois	1
24	Chickens	1
25	Cock	13
26	Cockatrice	4

27	Colt(s)	18
28	Coney; Conies	4
29	Cormorant	4
30	Crane	2
31	Creatures (general)	12
32	Cuckow	2
33	Deer	2
34	Dog(s)	41
35	Dove(s)	41
36	Dragon(s)	35
37	Dromedary; Dromedaries	4
38	Eagle(s)	34
39	Ewe	10
40	Fatling (general)	6
41	Ferret	1
42	Fish(es)	61
43	Flea	2
44	Flies	10
45	Flock(s)	187
46	Foal(s)	4
47	Fowl(s)	85
48	Fox(es)	9
49	Frogs	14
50	Gier	2
51	Glede	1
52	Gnat	1
53	Goat(s)	124
54	Grasshopper(s)	10
55	Greyhound	1
56	Hare	2
57	Hart(s)	11
58	Hawk	5
59	Heifer(s)	20
60	Hen	2
61	Hornet(s)	3
62	Horse(s)	150

63	Kite	2
64	Lamb(s)	166
65	Lapwing	2
66	Leopard(s)	8
67	Leviathan	5
68	Lion(s); Lioness	152
69	Lizard	1
70	Locust(s)	28
71	Mice; Mouse	6
72	Mole(s)	2
73	Monsters	1
74	Moth	11
75	Osprey	2
76	Ossifrage	2
77	Ostrich	2
78	Owl(s)	16
79	Ox; Oxen	153
80	Palmerworm	3
81	Partridge	2
82	Peacocks	3
83	Pelican	3
84	Pigeon(s)	11
85	Pygarg	1
86	Quail(s)	4
87	Ram(s)	145
88	Raven	6
89	Roebuck(s); Roe(s)	17
90	Scapegoat	4
91	Scorpion(s)	9
92	Serpent(s)	53
93	Sheep	286
94	Snail	2
95	Sparrow(s)	6
96	Spider(s)	3
97	Stork	5
98	Swallow	4

99	Swan	2
100	Swine	20
101	Tortoise	1
102	Turtledoves	5
103	Unicorn(s)	9
104	Viper(s)	109
105	Vulture(s)	4
106	Weasel	1
107	Whale	4
108	Whelp	13
109	Wolf; Wolves	13
110	Worm	21

Appendix 2

Major Animal Groupings		
A. Insects and Worms		
1. Ant	7. Flea	13. Moth
2. Ass (Donkey)	8. Fly	14. Palmerworm
3. Bee	9. Gnat	15. Scorpion
4. Beetle	10. Grasshopper	16. Snail
5. Cankerworm	11. Hornet	17. Spider
6. Caterpillar	12. Locust	18. Worm
B. Birds		
1. Birds (general)	12. Gier	23. Peacock
2. Bittern	13. Glede	24. Pelican
3. Brood (general)	14. Hawk	25. Pigeon
4. Chicken	15. Hen	26. Quail
5. Cock	16. Kite	27. Raven
6. Cormorant	17. Lapwing	28. Sparrow
7. Craine	18. Osprey	29. Stork
8. Cuckow	19. Ossifrage	30. Swallow
9. Dove	20. Ostrich	31. Swan
10. Eagle	21. Owl	32. Turtledove
11. Fowl (general)	22. Partridge	33. Vulture
C. Reptiles		
1. Adder	5. Cockatrice	9. Lizard
2. Asp	6. Dragon	10. Serpent
3. Behemoth	7. Frog	11. Tortoise
4. Chameleon	8. Leviathan	12. Viper
D. Mammals		
1. Ass	16. Dromedary	31. Lion/Lioness
2. Badger	17. Ewe	32. Mice/Mouse

3. Bats	18. Fatling	33. Mole
4. Bear	19. Ferret	34. Monster
5. Beast (general)	20. Flocks (general)	35. Ox/Oxen
6. Bull/Bullock	21. Foal	36. Pygarg
7. Calf/Calves	22. Fox	37. Ram
8. Camel	23. Goat	38. Roe/Roebuck
9. Cattle	24. Greyhound	39. Scapegoat
10. Chamois	25. Hare	40. Sheep
11. Colt	26. Hart	41. Swine
12. Coney	27. Heifer	42. Unicorn
13. Creatures (general)	28. Horse	43. Weasel
14. Deer	29. Lamb	44. Whale
15. Dog	30. Leopard	45. Whelp
		46. Wolf

Appendix 3

Scripture References by Animal

1. **Ass, Ass's, Asses**
    Genesis 12:16; 22:3, 5; 24:35; 30:43; 32:5, 15; 34:20, 28; 36:24; 42:26–27; 43:18.24: 44:3, 13; 45:23; 47:17; 49:11, 14;
    Exodus 4:20; 9:3; 13:13; 20:17; 21:33; 22:4, 9, 10; 23:4, 5, 12; 34:20;
    Numbers 16:15; 22:21–23, 25, 27–30, 32, 33; 31:28, 30, 34, 39, 45;
    Deuteronomy 5:14, 21; 22:3, 4, 10; 28:31;
    Joshua 6:21; 7:24; 9:4; 15:18;
    Judges 1:14; 5;10; 6:4; 10:4; 12:14; 15:15, 16; 19:3, 10, 19, 21, 28;
    1 Samuel 8:16; 9:3, 5, 20: 10:2, 14, 16; 12:3; 15:3; 16:20; 22;19; 23:42; 25:18, 20; 27:9;
    2 Samuel 16:1, 2; 17:23; 19:26;
    1 Kings 2:40; 13:13, 23, 24, 27–29;
    1 Chronicles 5:21; 12:40; 27:30;
    2 Chronicles 28:15;
    2 Kings 4:22, 24; 6:25; 7:7, 10;
    Ezra 2:67;
    Nehemiah 7:69; 13:15;
    Job 1:3, 14; 6:5; 11:12; 12:15; 24:3, 5; 39:5; 42:12;
    Psalm 104:11;
    Proverbs 26:3;
    Isaiah 1:3; 21:7; 30:6, 24; 32:14, 20;
    Jeremiah 2:24; 14:6; 22:19;

Ezekiel 23:20;
Daniel 5:21;
Hosea 8:9;
Zechariah 9:9; 14:15;
Matthew 21:2, 5, 7;
Luke 13:15, 4:5;
John 12:14, 15;
2 Peter 2:16.

2. **Bear**
    1 Samuel 17:34, 36, 37;
    2 Samuel 17:8;
    2 Kings 2:24;
    Proverbs 17:12; 28:15;
    Isaiah 11:7; 59:11;
    Lamentations 3:10;
    Daniel 7:5;
    Hosea 13:8;
    Revelation 13:2.

3. **Bee(s)**
    Deuteronomy 1:44;
    Judges 14:8;
    Psalm 118:12.

4. **Behemoth**
    Job 40:15.

5. **Bird(s), Bird's**
    Genesis 7:14; 15:10; 47:17, 19;
    Leviticus 14:4–7, 49–53;
    Deuteronomy 14:11;
    2 Samuel 21:10; Job 41:5;
    Psalm 11:1; 104:17; 124:7;
    Proverbs 1:17; 6:5; 7:23; 26:2; 27:8;
    Ecclesiastes 9:12; 10:20; 12:4;

Song of Solomon 2:12;
Isaiah 16:2; 31:5; 46:11;
Jeremiah 4:25; 5:27; 12:4, 9;
Lamentations 3:52;
Ezekiel 39:4;
Hosea 9:11; 11:11;
Amos 3:5;
Matthew 8:20; 13:32;
Luke 9:58;
Romans 1:23;
1 Corinthians 15:39;
James 3:7;
Revelation 18:2.

6. **Bittern**
Isaiah 14:23; 34:11;
Zephaniah 2:14.

7. **Cattle**
Genesis 1:24–26; 2:20; 3:14; 4:20; 6:20; 7:14, 21, 23; 8:1, 17; 9:10; 13:2, 7; 29:7; 30:29, 32, 39–43; 31:8–0, 12, 18, 41, 43; 33:14, 17; 34:5, 23; 36:6–7; 46:6, 32, 34; 47:6, 16–18;
Exodus 9:3–4, 6–7, 19–21; 10:26; 12:29, 38; 17:3; 20:10; 43:19;
Leviticus 1:2; 5:2; 19:19; 25:7; 26:22;
Numbers 3:41, 45; 20:4, 19; 31:9; 32:1, 4, 16, 26; 35:3;
Deuteronomy 2:35; 3:7, 19; 5:14; 7:14; 11:15; 13:15; 20:14; 28:4, 11, 51; 30:9;
Joshua 1:14; 8:2, 27; 11:14; 14:4; 21:2; 22:8;
Judges 6:5; 18:21;
1 Samuel 23:5; 30:20;
1 Kings 1:9, 19, 25;
2 Kings 3:9, 17;
1 Chronicles 5:9, 21; 7:21;
2 Chronicles 14:15; 26:10; 35:8–9;

Nehemiah 9:37; 10:36;
Job 36:33;
Psalm 50:10; 78:48; 104:14; 107:38; 148:10;
Ecclesiastes 2:7;
Isaiah 7:25; 30:23; 43:23; 46:1;
Jeremiah 9:10; 49:32;
Ezekiel 34:17, 20, 22; 38:12–13;
Joel 1:18;
Jonah 4:11;
Haggai 1:11;
Zechariah 2:4; 13:5;
Luke 17:7;
John 4:12.

8. **Chameleon**
   Leviticus 11:30.

9. **Deer**
   Deuteronomy 14:5.

10. **Fallow Deer**
    1 Kings 4:23.

11. **Hart(s)**
    Deuteronomy 12:15, 22; 14:5; 15:22;
    1 Kings 4:23;
    Psalm 42:1;
    Song of Solomon 2:9, 17; 8:14;
    Lamentations 1:6;
    Isaiah 35:6.

12. **Roe(s), Roebuck(s)**
    Deuteronomy 12:15, 22; 14:5; 15:22;
    2 Samuel 2:18;
    1 Kings 4:23;
    1 Chronicles 12:8;

Proverbs 5:19; 6:5;
Song of Solomon 2:7, 9, 17; 3:5; 4:5; 7:13; 8:14;
Isaiah 13:14.

13. **Dog, Dog's, Dogs**
Exodus 11:7; 22:31;
Deuteronomy 23:18;
Judges 7:5;
1 Samuel 17:43; 24:14;
2 Samuel 3:8; 9:8; 16:9;
1 Kings 14:11; 16:4; 21:19, 23–24; 22:38;
2 Kings 8:13; 9:10, 36;
Job 30:1;
Psalm 22:16, 20; 59:14; 68:23;
Proverbs 26:11, 17;
Ecclesiastes 9:4;
Isaiah 56:10–11; 66:3;
Jeremiah 15:3;
Matthew 7:6; 15:26, 27;
Mark 7:27–28;
Luke 18:21;
Philippians 3:2;
2 Peter 2:22;
Revelation 22:15.

14. **Eagle(s), Eagle's**
Exodus 19:4;
Leviticus 11:13, 18;
Deuteronomy 14:12, 17; 28:49; 32:11;
2 Samuel 1:23;
Job 9:26; 39:27;
Psalm 103:5;
Proverbs 23:5; 30:17, 19;
Isaiah 40:31;
Jeremiah 4:13; 48:40; 49:16, 22;
Lamentations 4:19;

Ezekiel 1:10; 10:14; 17:3, 7;
Daniel 4:33; 7:4;
Hosea 8:1;
Obadiah 4;
Micah 1:16;
Habakkuk 1:8;
Matthew 24:28;
Luke 17:37;
Revelation 4:7; 12:14.

15. **Flock(s)**
Genesis 4:4; 13:5; 21:28; 24:35; 26:14; 27:9; 29:2–3, 8, 10; 30:31–32, 36, 38, 40; 31:4, 32:5, 7; 33:13; 37:2, 12–14, 16; 38:17; 45:10; 46:32; 47:1, 4, 17; 50:8;
Exodus 2:16–17, 19; 3:1; 10:9, 24; 12:32, 38; 34:3;
Leviticus 1:2; 3:6, 10; 5:6, 15, 18; 6:6; 27:32;
Numbers 11;22; 15:3; 31:9, 24, 30; 32:26; 33:12–13; 49:29; 50:8;
Deuteronomy 7:13; 8:13; 12:6, 17, 21; 14:23; 15:14, 19; 16:2; 28:4, 51;
1 Samuel 17:34; 30:20;
2 Samuel 12:2, 4;
1 Kings 20:27;
1 Chronicles 4:39, 41; 27:31;
2 Chronicles 17:11; 32:28–29; 35:7;
Ezra 10:19;
Nehemiah 10:36;
Job 21:11; 24:2; 30:1;
Psalm 65:13; 77:20; 78:48, 52; 80:1; 107:41;
Proverbs 27:23;
Song of Solomon 1:7–8; 4:1–2; 6:5–6;
Isaiah 10:11; 17:2; 32:14; 60:7; 61:5; 63:11; 65:10;
Jeremiah 3:24; 5:17; 6:3; 10:21; 13:17, 20; 23:2–3; 25:34–36; 31:10, 12; 49:20; 50:45; 51:23;
Ezekiel 24:5; 34:2, 3, 6, 8, 10, 12, 15, 17, 19, 22, 31; 36:37–38; 43:23; 45:15;

Hosea 5:6;
Joel 1:18;
Amos 6:4; 7:15;
Jonah 3:7;
Micah 2:12; 4:8; 5:8; 7:14;
Zephaniah 2:6, 14;
Habakkuk 3:17;
Zechariah 9:16; 10:2–3; 11:4, 7, 11, 17;
Malachi 1:14;
Matthew 26:31;
Luke 2:8; 12:32;
Acts 20:28–29;
1 Corinthians 9:7;
1 Peter 5:2–3.

16. **Giraffe**
No scriptural references found.

17. **Gnat**
Matthew 23:24.

18. **Hawk**
Leviticus 11:16;
Deuteronomy 14:15;
Job 39:26.

19. **Herd(s)**
Genesis 13:5; 18:7; 24:35; 26:14; 32:7; 33:13; 45:10;
    46:32; 47:1, 17, 18; 50:8;
Exodus 10:9, 24; 12:32, 38; 34:3;
Leviticus 1:2–3; 3:1;
Numbers 11:22; 15:3;
Deuteronomy 8:13; 12: 6, 17, 21; 14:23; 15:19; 16:2;
1 Samuel 11:5; 30:20;
2 Samuel 12:2, 4;
1 Chronicles 27:29;

2 Chronicles 32:29;
Nehemiah 10:36;
Proverbs 27:23;
Isaiah 65:10;
Jeremiah 3:24; 5:17; 31:12;
Hosea 5:6;
Joel 1:18;
Jonah 3:7;
Habakkuk 3:17;
Matthew 8:30–32;
Mark 5:11, 13;
Luke 8:32–33.

20. **Horse(s), Horses'**
Genesis 47:17; 49:17;
Exodus 9:13; 14:9, 23; 15:1, 19, 21;
Deuteronomy 11:4; 17:16; 20:1;
Joshua 11:4, 6, 9; 2;
Samuel 15:1;
1 Kings 4:26, 28; 10:25, 28–29; 18:5; 20:1, 21, 25; 22:4;
2 Kings 2:11; 3:7; 5:9; 6:14–5, 17; 7:6–7, 10, 13–14; 9:33;
    10:2; 11:16; 14:20; 18:23; 23:11;
1 Chronicles 18:4;
2 Chronicles 1:16–17; 9:24–25, 28; 23:15; 25:28;
Ezra 2:66;
Nehemiah 3:28; 7:68;
Esther 6:8–11;
Job 39:18, 19;
Psalm 20:7; 32:9; 33:17; 76:6; 147:10;
Proverbs 21:31;
Ecclesiastes 10:7;
Song of Solomon 1:9; 26:3;
Isaiah 2:7; 30:16; 31:1, 3; 36:8; 43:17; 63:13; 66:20;
Jeremiah 4:13; 5:8; 6:23; 8:6, 16; 12:5; 17:25; 22:4; 31:40;
    46:4, 9; 47:3; 50:37, 42; 51:21, 27;

Ezekiel 17:15; 23:6, 12, 20, 23; 26:7, 10–11; 27:14; 38:4, 15; 39:20;
Hosea 1:7; 14:3;
Joel 2:4;
Amos 2:15; 4:10; 6:12;
Micah 5:10;
Nahum 3:2;
Zechariah 1:8, 18; 6:2–3, 6; 9:10; 10:3, 5; 12:4; 14:15, 20;
Revelation 6:2, 4–5, 8; 9:7, 9, 17; 14:20; 18:13; 19:11, 14, 18–19, 21.

21. **Owl(s)**
Leviticus 11:16, 17;
Deuteronomy 14:15–16;
Job 30:29;
Psalm 102:6;
Isaiah 13:21; 34:11, 13–15;
Jeremiah 50:39;
Micah 1:8.

22. **Ox, Oxen**
Genesis 12:16; 20:14; 21:27; 32:5; 34:28;
Exodus 9:3; 20:17, 24; 21:28–29, 32–33, 35–36; 22:1, 4, 9–10; 23:4, 12; 24:5; 34:19;
Leviticus 7:23; 17:3; 27:26;
Numbers 7:3, 6–8; 17:23, 29, 35, 41, 47, 53, 59, 65, 71, 77, 83, 87–88; 22:4, 40; 23:11;
Deuteronomy 5:14, 21; 14:4–5, 26 18:3; 22:1, 4, 10; 25:4; 28:31;
Joshua 6:21; 7:24;
Judges 3:31; 6:4;
1 Samuel 11:7; 12:3; 14:14, 32, 34; 15:3;9, 14–15, 21; 22:19; 27:9;
2 Samuel 6:6, 13; 24:22, 24;
1 Kings 9, 19, 25; 4:23; 7:25, 29, 44; 8:5, 63; 19:19–21;
2 Kings 5:26; 16:17;

1 Chronicles 12:40; 13:9; 21:23;
2 Chronicles 4:3–4, 15; 5:6; 7:5; 15:11; 18:2; 29:33; 31:6;
    35:8–9, 12;
Nehemiah 5:18;
Job 1:3, 14; 6:5; 24:3; 40:15; 42:12;
Psalm 8:7; 69:31; 106:20; 144:14;
Proverbs 7:22; 14:4; 15:17;
Isaiah 1:3; 7:25; 11:7; 22:13; 30:24; 32:20; 66:3;
Jeremiah 11:19; 51:23;
Ezekiel 1:10;
Daniel 4:25, 33; 5:21;
Amos 6:12;
Matthew 22:4;
Luke 13:15; 14:5, 19;
John 2:14–15;
Acts 14:13;
1 Corinthians 9:9;
1 Timothy 5:18.

23. **Peacocks**
    1 Kings 10:22;
    2 Chronicles 9:21;
    Job 39:13.

24. **Pigeon(s)**
    Genesis 15:9;
    Leviticus 1:14; 5:7, 11; 12:6, 8; 14:22, 30; 15:14, 29;
    Numbers 6:10;
    Luke 2:24.

25. **Quail**
    Exodus 16:13;
    Numbers 11:31–32;
    Psalm 105:40.

26. **Serpent, Serpent's, Serpents'**
Genesis 3:1, 2, 4, 13, 14; 49:17;
Exodus 4:3; 7:9, 10, 12, 15;
Numbers 21:6–9;
Deuteronomy 8:15; 32:24;
2 Kings 18:4;
Job 26:13;
Psalm 58:4; 140:3;
Proverbs 23:32; 30:19;
Ecclesiastes 10:8, 11;
Isaiah 14:29; 27:1; 30:6;
Jeremiah 8:17; 46:22;
Amos 5:19; 9:3;
Micah 7:17;
Matthew 7:10; 10:16; 23:33;
Mark 16:18;
Luke 10:19; 11:11;
John 3:14;
1 Corinthians 10:9;
2 Corinthians 11:3;
James 3:7;
Revelation 9:19; 12:9, 14, 15; 20:2.

27. **Adder, Adders'**
Genesis 49:17;
Psalm 58:4; 91:13; 140:3.

28. **Asp, Asps**
Deuteronomy 32:33;
Job 20:14, 16;
Isaiah 11:8;
Romans 3:13.

29. **Viper, Viper's, Vipers**
Job 20:16;
Isaiah 30:6; 59:5;

Matthew 3:7; 12:34; 23:33;
Luke 3:7;
Acts 28:3.

30. **Sheep**
Genesis 4:2; 12:16; 20:14; 21:27; 29:2–3, 6–0; 30:32–33,
35; 31:19; 34:28; 38:13;
Exodus 9:3; 12:5; 20:24; 22:1, 4, 9–10, 30; 34:19;
Leviticus 1:10; 7:23; 22:19, 21, 27; 27:26;
Numbers 18:17; 22:40; 27:17; 31:28, 32, 36–37, 43;
32:24, 36;
Deuteronomy 7:13; 14:4, 26; 15:19; 17:1; 18:3–4; 22:1;
28:4, 18, 31, 51; 32:14;
Joshua 6:21; 7:24; Judges 6:4;
1 Samuel 8:17; 14:32, 34; 5:3, 9, 14, 15, 21; 16:11, 19;
17:15, 20, 28, 34; 22:19; 25:2, 4, 16, 18; 27:9;
2 Samuel 7:8; 17:29; 24:17;
1 Kings 1:9, 19, 25; 4:23; 8:5, 63; 22:17;
2 Kings 5:26;
1 Chronicles 5:21; 12:40; 17:7; 21:17;
2 Chronicles 5:6; 7:5; 14:15; 15:11; 18:2, 16; 29:33; 30:24;
31:6;
Nehemiah 3:1, 32; 5:18; 12:39;
Job 1:3, 16; 31:20; 42:12;
Psalm 8:7; 44:11, 22; 49:14; 74:1; 78:52; 79:13; 95:7;
100:3; 119:176; 144:13;
Song of Solomon 4:2; 6:6;
Isaiah 7:21; 13:14; 22:13; 53:6–7;
Jeremiah 12:3; 23:1; 50:6, 17;
Ezekiel 34:6, 11–12;
Hosea 12:12; Joel 1:18;
Micah 2:12; 5:8;
Zechariah 13:7;
Matthew 9:36; 10:6, 16; 12:11–12; 15:24; 18:12–13;
25:32–33; 26:31;
Mark 6:34; 14:27;

Luke 15:4, 6;
John 2:14–5; 5:2; 10:2–4, 7–8, 11–16, 26–27; 21:16–17;
Acts 8:32;
Romans 8:36;
Hebrews 13:20;
1 Peter 2:25;
Revelation 18:13.

31. **Spider**
Job 8:14;
Proverbs 30:28;
Isaiah 59:5.

32. **Stork**
Leviticus 11:19;
Deuteronomy 14:18;
Psalm 104:17;
Jeremiah 8:7;
Zechariah 5:9.

33. **Tortoise**
Leviticus 11:29.

34. **Unicorn(s)**
Numbers 23:22; 24:8;
Deuteronomy 33:17;
Job 39:9–10;
Psalm 22:21; 29:6; 92:10;
Isaiah 34:7.

35. **Wolf, Wolves**
Genesis 49:27;
Ezekiel 22:27;
Isaiah 11:6; 65:25;
Jeremiah 5:6;
Habakkuk 1:8;

Zephaniah 3:3;
Matthew 7:15; 10:16;
Luke 10:3;
John 10:12;
Acts 20:29.

The scriptural references found in appendix 3 are all taken from *The Exhaustive Concordance of the Bible* by James Strong (MacDonald Publishing Company; McLean, Virginia).

About the Author

Ben grew up on a small family farm in western Pennsylvania where he was active in 4-H. He received his bachelor's degree in agricultural science from Penn State University in 1984, focusing on plant and animal science. He did a four-month agricultural internship at Heifer International Livestock Ranch in Arkansas as part of his college experience and was a member of the Penn State Livestock Judging Team. Ben went on to work for thirty-two years for Maryland Department of Agriculture as an agriculture resource conservation specialist. As an avid beekeeper, he teaches beekeeping courses at Allegany College of Maryland and mentors others.

"I cannot remember a time where I wasn't in church. It is an essential part of who I am." He was saved at the age of twelve and attends and serves on the board at Cumberland Bible Church. He graduated from the Cornerstone Bible Institute in 1996 and has been on multiple short-term mission trips to the Caribbean islands of St. Lucia and St. Kitts. Ben helps lead a weeklong family camp at Jumonville where he has attended for over fifty years.

"My faith in God has been put to the test as a double cancer survivor. It was after my second diagnosis that I felt compelled to get serious about writing this book. It helped me take the focus and worry off of me and on to something far more important. As you read *All Nature Sings*, I hope you can hear God resonating through the pages."

You can correspond with the author by emailing him at cooperville@atlanticbb.net

CPSIA information can be obtained
at www.ICGtesting.com
Printed in the USA
BVHW080043230219
540987BV00001B/5/P